COMPANIONS OF CHRIST

COMPANIONS OF CHRIST

Ignatian Spirituality for Everyday Living

Margaret Silf

WILLIAM B. EERDMANS PUBLISHING COMPANY
GRAND RAPIDS, MICHIGAN / CAMBRIDGE, U.K.

First published 2004 in the U.K. by
The Canterbury Press Norwich
a publishing imprint of
Hymns Ancient & Modern Limited,
a registered charity

This edition published 2005 in the United States of America by
Wm. B. Eerdmans Publishing Co.
2140 Oak Industrial Drive N.E., Grand Rapids, Michigan 49505 /
P.O. Box 163, Cambridge CB3 9PU U.K.

Printed in the United States of America

13 12 11 10 09 08   8 7 6 5 4 3

ISBN 978-0-8028-2942-9

www.eerdmans.com

Contents

Preface

When a stray cannon-ball shatters the knee of a Spanish soldier in a fortress in Northern Spain in the early sixteenth century it can knock you off your perch in the leafy suburbs of an English town, five centuries later.

The quantum physicists would say 'we told you so', but still it comes as a shock when it actually happens. It happened to me back in the 1970s, when I first felt drawn to find out more about Ignatius of Loyola and his famous *Exercises*. At the time I didn't know what I was doing, or what I was letting myself in for. Had I known what a goldmine of spiritual wisdom I was tapping into, I would have started much, much earlier!

I guess Inigo has accompanied me (probably shaking his head in dismay most of the time) ever since then in one way or another – alongside me when I was still fairly unquestioning of received Church doctrine and organization, but still not abandoning me when some of the old certainties began to crumble and I found myself walking in uncharted terrain. Thank God, Ignatian spirituality lets you do that – explore God and God's ways for yourself, discover for yourself what it all means for you, and how you want to respond to the call of Christ in your life, whether within, or beyond the boundaries that we traditionally call 'Church'.

Companionship has been a very important part of this journey. Through Inigo's wisdom I learned what it might mean to enter at a personal level into the life of the man Jesus, and there to discover the power of the Cosmic Christ. And through the companionship of some of Inigo's spiritual sons, contemporary Jesuits, I have been challenged to keep on deepening this journey and, in my turn, to share its power with others. I especially acknowledge the loving and faithful companionship I have shared through the years with Gerard Hughes SJ and Brian McClorry SJ, and the inspiration and encouragement I have been given by Fintan Creavan SJ, Michael Ivens SJ, Tom McGuinness SJ, Paul Nicholson SJ, and all members of the communities at St Beuno's and Loyola Hall, and by John Veltri SJ in Canada and Thomas Clarke SJ in the USA. I am also deeply grateful for the soul-friendship of countless other pilgrims, walking a similar path, whose lives have touched mine with God's own love.

'Discover for yourself', and then share the treasure with others – indeed this encapsulates so much of what Ignatian spirituality is about. It is about drinking deeply from the wells of our own lived experience, and sharing this living water with each other and the world. One way in which these two ideals come together is in the journey of prayer we might choose to make in the form of a retreat, which offers an opportunity to reflect on what is going on in our own lives, and how God is active in it, and then to share these reflections with a companion. The companion is there *only* to accompany, not to direct or to instruct, nor to 'fix' anything. It is like taking a walk through countryside that is full of surprises. The companion is there to be alongside; someone to share the surprises with and reflect on their meanings. He or she is there to *listen,* and, in response to what is being shared, at most to suggest some possibilities for the next day's 'walk'. This is the ethos underlying the experience of an 'Ignatian retreat'.

One very effective way of making a retreat is in the midst of our daily life, and my first encounter with Bishop Graham Chadwick was in just such a daily life retreat. I had freshly completed a training course in the skills of accompanying others on their journey with God, and had been asked to join the team facilitating a retreat in daily life, on Merseyside. Bishop Graham was supervising this retreat, and we nervous 'prayer companions' sat on the edge of our chairs as he expertly introduced the retreat and explained how it would be conducted. Then he asked if there were any questions. One of the retreatants raised his hand. 'I want to ask the prayer companions what makes them think they can teach us to pray,' he announced. We all swallowed hard, and stared at the ground, waiting for Bishop Graham's response. 'Well,' he asked, as he fielded the question deftly in our direction, 'what do the prayer companions think?' I had a kind of déjà vu when he asked me to write this book – challenging me once again to leave my comfort zone and explore some of my own ever-expanding questions and the ever-growing answers that God keeps on providing.

Ignatian spirituality has this knack of turning the questions back to ourselves, and so I make no apology for doing exactly that now with you – by inviting you into your own journey of discovery. Who is this Ignatius Loyola, and why would his *Spiritual Exercises* have anything to say to you in your twenty-first-century life? May the curiosity that has led you this far now encourage you to journey on . . . but beware of speeding cannon-balls.

I

Inigo – the Man Behind the Myth

Probably the last thing Inigo Lopez would have wanted, I venture to suggest, at least in his more mature years, would have been to become something of a cult figure for spiritual searchers in subsequent centuries. The best gurus, indeed, are usually those who deny any such role and resist every attempt to put them on a pedestal. Even so, this man is interesting, and his life is quite an adventure, in more ways than one. Moreover, the particular approach to Christian spirituality that is his special contribution has become widely explored in recent times, both within and beyond the visible 'church'. So I hope he will forgive us if we indulge in a bit of creative nostalgia, and imagine ourselves back in the Basque country of Northern Spain, some five hundred years ago.

There is a purpose in the exercise. We will peer back through the lenses of history not just out of curiosity (though Inigo's story justifies a certain amount of healthy curiosity), but also with a view to finding something of our own story reflected back from that, now slightly antiquated, mirror. It is a bit like rummaging through grandmother's attic and discovering old newspapers that, quite startlingly, have something very relevant to say about today's world and our place in it. When we rummage around in Inigo's attic, we find there are treasures there that stop us in our tracks with their spot-on insights into some of our most pressing spiritual questions in the twenty-first century. But don't take my word for it . . . decide for yourself.

If I had to summarize in a sentence what Ignatian spirituality means for me, I would certainly want to include two keywords in that sentence: 'story' and 'image'.

The story-telling aspect of Ignatian spirituality speaks to us today, especially by invoking our intuitive sense of being engaged in a process, or a journey, rather than being cogs in a fixed system or structure. Perhaps that is because Inigo himself discovered so much wisdom, not from 'the system', but from his own direct experience of God's action in his life and the process of growth that this action initiated and nourished.

The use of image in the Ignatian approach is rooted in his recommendation that we indeed use our imagination in prayer – in ways that we will explore later in this book. For many, this way of praying has opened up fresh new possibilities of discovering the real, living connections between the gospel story and their own stories, which is often the first step to embodying gospel values in our own choices and decisions.

Given these two key aspects of Ignatian spirituality, it seems appropriate to begin our exploration by entering a little into Inigo's own story, and by pausing to reflect on a few snapshot images from that story which may reveal something of what it is that gives Ignatian spirituality its particular flavour and character. To do this, we must travel back in time in two ways:

• Back to incidents that happened in Northern Spain, Rome and Paris at the beginning of the sixteenth century;
• Back to our own personal memory bank.

I invite you to browse through the photo album with me for a few minutes, and pause to reflect, not only on what these snapshots reveal of Inigo, but also the ways in which they resonate with your own story.

A Basque boy

Our first picture is of a little boy born in 1491, the youngest of 12 children. The place is a sunny spot in the Basque region of Northern Spain, and the family seat of this noble family is at the castle of Loyola. This is where Inigo spends his early years, and seems destined for an aristocratic life and a military or courtly career. His formal training begins at the age of 14, preparing to be a royal page to the King of Spain.

The boy grows to young manhood, and at the age of 22 experiences redundancy, on the death of his employer, Don Juan Valasquez, who had ensured his favour with the royal court. With Valasquez, Inigo's income and status die too. His next employer is the Duke of Najera. Inigo works as a 'gentleman-at-arms' and begins serious military training. He is full of the zeal of his class, certainly not immune to the attractions of women, nor above the odd street brawl when he is crossed. It hardly seems like the best nursery for a future saint, but God writes straight with crooked lines.

As you ponder Inigo's youth, how do you feel about your own? Perhaps you have no regrets. Or perhaps you can't see, even with hindsight, where on earth God was in all your struggles to grow up and shape a life for yourself. Just notice what you see, and stow it away in your inner album, without any judgement. Remember, God writes straight with crooked lines.

Wounded hero

The next snapshot takes us back to a completely forget-
table, and largely forgotten battle around the Spanish
fortification of Pamplona. The battle is raging between the
French and the Spanish. Inigo Lopez of Loyola is defending
the fortress, with more courage than common sense,
against an overwhelming French invasion. We find him
standing there, bold and determined, defying the inevitable.
His hour on the parapets is to be short, however. It ends
when a cannon-ball shatters his leg and breaks his knee.
And along with his knee, the cannon-ball shatters his ambition, his pride, his dreams and his self-esteem. It lays him
low. It puts him radically out of action.

Without a doubt it was the personal catastrophe of
Pamplona that became the means through which God
worked his miracle in Inigo. But Inigo's story and his
subsequent experience of working it out in his life is only of
value to us because it catches some of the threads of the
universal pilgrim story.

Spain's loss was to become Inigo's gain, in the long term.
And God's gain, and ours too. And isn't it true that the deep
and life-changing movements in our story so often happen
when we are floored and floundering, hapless and helpless?

So perhaps the problems that we so long to circumvent or
the pain we seek to avoid may be the very places where we
are being drawn *beyond* ourselves. They may be the very
places that stretch us towards new understanding, deeper
love – the places that contain the seeds of our growth.

Is there any part of your life, or your story, that reminds
you of the Pamplona experience – times when you have
acted with courage or even with recklessness, or times
when you have been 'laid low', and felt helpless and a
failure? How do you feel about those things now?

The dreamer

Inigo's career as a soldier had ended in defeat, humiliation and extreme pain. Reputation, strength, status, ambition – all those things were gone in the moment it took the cannon-ball to shatter his knee. He finds himself with plenty of time to brood on these things, as he is carried across the mountains on a stretcher, back to the family home in Loyola, there to spend months trying to recover from an injury that nearly cost him his life.

In all of this there is still no sign of God making a dramatic entrance into this wounded soldier's life. Rather the opposite, in fact. Inigo can't have been the easiest patient. As soon as he can find enough energy to read a book, he casts around in the Loyola library for some literature to while away the boredom. He wants something to engage his imagination. He finds more than he has bargained for, in a surprising quarter. Learning that the library doesn't have his favourite romantic novels or adventure stories, he has to make do with a life of Christ and lives of the saints. His comments on first being offered this fare are not recorded!

An active mind is not an easy tenant of an immobilized body. Our third snapshot reveals Inigo in the process of relieving his boredom – by daydreaming. Perhaps first as an escape route from the lives of the saints, he spends his time fantasizing about the fine ladies he would like to pursue and the great battles he would like to win. This is fine as long as the dream lasts, but he realizes that it leaves him feeling more disgruntled than ever. He even gets to wondering *why* it should leave him so flat and dejected. Perhaps it is because it is all history now, and this injury has put him out of the league when it comes to women and glory. Or could it also be because these dreams are all centred on Inigo, and Inigo is no longer centre stage. Maybe his disappointment and frustration with himself is penetrating his daydreams, and colouring them grey?

But there are other dreams. The life of Christ and the lives of the saints don't leave him untouched after all. He starts to dream about doing the saint-thing himself. If men like Francis and Dominic could do great things, why not Inigo? So off he goes into dreamland again, this time imagining himself giving his all, as they had done, for a cause that is worth spending a life for. And he notices that this kind of dreaming has a different effect on him, leaving him inspired and more alive, his inner energy store replenished and overflowing. The King of Spain is not, after all, the last word in kings. There is another King, whose service engaged the minds and hearts of these fine men in the past. That same King is already knocking on the door of Inigo's own heart, with a call and a challenge that is going to shape every moment of his life from now on.

Inigo's discovery of this difference in the after-effects of his dreams is the beginning of *discernment*. He begins to notice which dreams are capable of sustaining him and providing new vision and energy, and which dreams are transitory, leaving him feeling flat and disappointed. It is the start of a personal experience and understanding of the inner movements going on all the time in his mind and heart. He begins to notice his moods and feelings and reactions, and to measure them against this unseen compass of discernment. And gradually his desire begins to grow for what sustains him and gives him life, and he becomes more willing and able to let go of what is not (or is no longer) leading to life. He is learning how to distinguish between his own self-focused fantasies, and the stirrings of what we might call the God-dream within him.

Can you recognize, and name, any of your 'day-dreams'? What do you hope for, in your wildest dreams? What have you hoped for and dreamed of in earlier stages of your life? Have any of these daydreams become 'God-dreams' – that is, visions capable of releasing new energy in you and possibly changing the direction of your life?

Mountain high . . .

Inigo has experienced a radical conversion during his painful period of convalescence in the castle at Loyola. He is ready, and eager, to live out the God-dream and to make it incarnate in his own life. He sets off from Loyola, a pilgrim for God.

Our next snapshot records Inigo's pilgrimage in search of the deepest desire of his heart. And we find him, first, at the Abbey of Montserrat, high on a jagged mountain peak, overlooking the plain of Manresa. Here, in the abbey, he makes his confession (which tradition tells us took all of three days!) and receives his first guidance in prayer.

By any standards, the jagged teeth of the Montserrat mountains are spectacular. It is in this dramatic setting that Inigo lives his spiritual mountain-top experience. This is the time of commitment. He marks this crucial decision – his 'option for God' – with a typically impulsive gesture. He gives his fine nobleman's clothes to a beggar, and dons the simple outfit of a poor traveller. (The beggar is later arrested on suspicion of having stolen the clothes!) And he places his sword and dagger on the altar as a sign of surrender of all that he had valued in the past, and a symbol of his new commitment to the service of God.

Can you look back on times in your life when you were fired by the highest ideals, and ready to give up everything to pursue the dreams of your heart? Can you identify with the impulsive Inigo, overflowing with his new-found love of God and eager to show the depth of his commitment? Remember your own 'mountain-top experiences' and the feelings you experienced in them. How do you feel about the way those dreams have worked out?

Inigo leaves his sword and dagger behind on the altar at Montserrat, as a symbolic and actual surrender of his former life. What might you want to leave behind in your personal 'Montserrat', perhaps because it is hampering your onward journey, or no longer reflects your deepest desire in life? What defences would you like to let go, if only you had the courage? Do you know what is holding you back?

Don't make any kind of judgement, either of yourself or of others. Simply allow yourself to become aware of how you are feeling and what you really desire.

. . . and valley deep

We all know how hard it can be to come 'down to earth' again after a heightened spiritual experience. Yet if the commitment is to become a reality in our lives, we have to bring it down to where our lives are really being lived. For Inigo, this means coming down from the high drama of Montserrat to the plain of Manresa, intending to stay there for 'a few days' before going on to Barcelona, where he hopes to board a boat to the Holy Land. These 'few days' stretch into eleven months, and it is in Manresa where the next stage of Inigo's pilgrimage is to take shape, and in a manner very, very different from anything he had planned or expected.

Determined to live true to all that he has promised God up in Montserrat, the proud and self-willed Inigo now faces the heat and dust of everyday reality. Our next snapshot reveals him begging for his food and coming face to face with the dark side of the dream. He makes a 'home' for himself in a cave near the river. Alone, in this bleak place, he begins to meet his own 'demons'. Here the insights of his dream-time in Loyola are put to the test in the cold light of day. He is to discover for himself the true force of the 'destructive spirits' of spiritual desolation as well as the overwhelming joy that only the 'creative spirits' of spiritual consolation can bring.

In the Manresa months, Inigo is, as it were, living in his personal wilderness, which exposes him to the extremes of his own personality, as well as to the depths of God's love. There in his cave, he experiences the very best of himself and the very worst. The worst leads him close to suicide. The best leads him close to God. He begins to notice the dynamic of God's love operating in his heart, and to realize that when his focus is on himself, and his past and present failures and sinfulness, real or imagined, the destructive movements are likely to overwhelm him and paralyze all his efforts for good. When his focus is on God, however, and on the world around him with all its needs and longings, he notices that the creative movements within him will restore him to the sense of vocation that has led him this far on his journey.

His own moods – reflectors of those hidden inner movements, the God-focused joy and the self-focused despair – help him to find his way forward, by trial and error, on his inner journey to God. He learns how to use his feelings and reactions, and his memories and desires, as pointers to help him to seek out what, in every situation, is leading him closer to God and to leave aside anything that is causing him to drift away from God.

And as he journeys through this huge inner struggle, he records his experience in a notebook which forms the basis of his *Spiritual Exercises*. These notes have helped countless thousands of pilgrims, through the centuries, to uncover their own hidden depths in the search for God, and we will explore them more fully in a later chapter.

Remember again any 'mountain-top experiences' when you felt very close to God and full of enthusiasm and inspiration. Now recall the descent 'back to the plain'. How did you feel as you made that descent? Were you able to carry any of the joy and the grace of the mountain-top back to your life on the plain?

Imagine your own personal 'Manresa' – perhaps your present circumstances, where you are trying to discern God's leading in your life. Where are the dark areas (the destructive movements)? Where do you feel you are focused upon yourself and your own shortcomings or achievements? Where are the shafts of light (the creative movements) – the new visions, the inspirations? Where are they leading you? How might you encourage and further them? Are the dark experiences teaching you anything, or leading to new growth?

Back to school and a summer picnic

Be prepared for a surprise when you leaf over the next two snapshots. After the heights of Montserrat and the depths of Manresa, the pilgrim might well have hoped for an uncomplicated life in the service of God, sharing the fruits of his own experience with others. It was not to be. It very rarely is! So we join him now following a series of setbacks and disappointments, including the frustration of his dreams of serving God in the Holy Land, ill health, a close shave in a shipwreck, and some major opposition to his ministry which leads him into the grip of the Inquisition. How can this upstart layman be preaching the gospel, when he hasn't been to seminary? Who knows what he might be up to! Secular and Church authorities alike set themselves against him, but his determination only deepens to serve God in the face of whatever opposition and humiliation may come his way.

This leads him to a surprising new idea. If the only way to be accepted as a credible authority in the Church of his time is to be ordained, then this is what he will do. And so our next snapshot reveals the grown Inigo sitting uncomfortably at a school desk, among a gaggle of twelve-year-olds, learning Latin, with a 'whatever it takes' expression on his furrowed brow.

Eventually Latin is conquered, school yields to university, and Inigo is off to study in Paris. There, as elsewhere, he freely offers his companions the benefit of his spiritual experience in Manresa, in the form of his *Spiritual Exercises*. Particular friends are Francis Xavier and Peter Favre, whose lives are changed by the power of the sustained prayer of the *Exercises* and who long, like Inigo, to share the experience more widely. By 1534 the band of friends has grown to seven, and our next snapshot finds them out for a summer picnic on 15 August 1534. It was a celebration picnic. They have just shared the Eucharist, and made solemn vows that they will serve God together as companions of Christ, or in Latin, *Socii Jesu*, a religious order which has come to be known as the Society of Jesus, or the Jesuits. Surely the Jesuits must be the only religious order to have launched itself with a picnic in a Paris park.

> Remember any setbacks or opposition you have experienced in your own desire to live true to yourself and to God. Without any judgement, just let them be there, and notice how you have eventually moved beyond them, perhaps in ways that you could never have foreseen.
>
> Who are your special human companions in the quest for God? How do you express this special friendship – perhaps by meeting regularly, or writing, or sharing your faith together in a deep way?

Living the vision

The next snapshot captures a scene on the road to Rome. Inigo has been ordained now (in 1536), and taken the name Ignatius. His desire has deepened; he longs to be close to Christ in a very specific way. In his *Autobiography* we learn that he expresses this desire in the form of a request to Mary, begging her to 'place me with your Son'.

We find him at a church still a few miles away from the city, in a place called La Storta, where he has stopped to pray. Underneath this prayer, surely, lies his deep desire to be placed with the Lord. Whatever may be in his mind as he prays there in the church at La Storta, he is suddenly flooded by an overwhelming awareness of God's presence. This is how he describes it in the *Autobiography*:

> One day, while still a few miles from Rome, he was praying in a church and experienced such a change in his soul

and saw so clearly that God the Father had placed him with His Son Christ that he could not doubt that God the Father had indeed placed him with His Son.

Is this just a personal phenomenon that we cannot explain, but must simply accept? Is it something utterly remote from our own experience of God? Is it a nine-days wonder that will fade in the light of 'normal' life? All we can say is that this visionary experience clearly becomes pivotal for Ignatius through the remainder of his life. We can 'test' it, if we wish, against the question 'Did it make a difference?' And perhaps we might test our own felt experiences of God's presence in the same kind of way: do they make a *difference* to the way we live and relate to others?

Ignatius feels that his prayer has been answered. Sometimes we might feel, too, that God has answered prayer in ways we didn't expect, and we don't rightly know what to do with the answer. Perhaps this is how Ignatius feels. He had asked to be placed with Christ, and now feels that this has, somehow, mysteriously happened. What would this mean in practice? What does it mean to be a companion of Jesus in this intimate way? Is it something that we desire ourselves? Or do we perhaps feel afraid of it?

People making the Ignatian *Exercises* frequently pray for a particular 'grace', as Ignatius urges us to do. They may, for example, be consistently praying for the grace to be close to Jesus in his suffering and death. As they reflect on their experience of living their daily lives in a painful world, they may become aware of whole tracts of loneliness in their lives, or they may share their feelings about a situation in which they have felt 'put down' or sidelined or even actively opposed. Often they do not, immediately, realize the connection between these very specific experiences in their own lives, and the prayer they have been making to be close to Jesus in his.

The breakthrough when they make the connection can be extraordinarily powerful, and the beginning of the realization that Christ's redeeming, atoning work is now being lived out *in our own lives* as we work and pray for the coming of the Kingdom. The grace they have asked for has been given, and perhaps there are times when they wish they had never asked for it!

In the light of Ignatius's visionary experience at La Storta, reflect on one or more of your own personal moments of vision. Get in touch with a moment in your life that has lit you up with new understanding or a new direction or purpose. How do you feel you have lived out this moment, and let its joy and its energy become part of who you are? Has it made a lasting difference to you or to those around you?

Earthing the dream

Visionary experiences are all very well, but they only become incarnate when they are lived out in practice. How can Ignatius help us to find ways of doing this?

Three ways in particular are very close to the heart of Ignatian spirituality:

- Nurturing an intimate relationship with Jesus by praying the Gospels in a personal, and perhaps imaginative way. In Gospel meditation, we consciously seek to connect our own lives and decisions with the events and teaching of Jesus' earthly ministry. The more we are able to do this, the more we will imbibe his values and integrate them into our own lives. It becomes possible to say, as we name and acknowledge our own personal circumstances and situations, 'In my life right now, Christ is wanting to become incarnate in what it means to be . . .' Each of us will complete this sentence in our own way.

- Letting contemplation turn to action, by putting into effect in our lives what we are discovering in our prayer. What is given in prayer is never given for one alone, but for all. The challenge is to discover the specific ways in which God is calling you to express God's love uniquely in your life – and then to turn your discovery into real and specific action. As we live our lives and, perhaps, develop the habit of reflecting back each day over where we feel God has been present to us in the day, and where God may have been nudging us or challenging us, we can then begin to put these Gospel values into action in the way we make our choices.

- We can participate very fully in one of the ways in which Ignatius lived out his inner vision in a practical apostolate, which is particularly relevant to us today as a pilgrim people in a secular world: the art of spiritual conversation and spiritual companionship. How does this work for us today? What opportunities are available to us? What might we do to exercise this gentle ministry in practice?

And a 'gentle', yet powerful, ministry is what it is. Now, five centuries after the beginnings of the Ignatian tradition and the founding of the Jesuits, we look back over a chequered history. For many people the very word 'Jesuit' evokes images of fiery warriors of the Counter-Reformation, defending a sometimes indefensible Roman Catholic structure against the challenges of renewal and growth. Indeed the Society of Jesus has sometimes been called the Vatican's fire brigade. This is a sad misrepresentation, when applied to today's Jesuits. Far from reinforcing repressive practices, they have, in the late twentieth and early twenty-first centuries, become a powerful force for change and renewal both within and beyond the Roman Catholic Church. They are pioneers in the fields of ecumenism, the education of the young, the empowerment of women in the Church, the nurturing of lay and collaborative ministry, the provision of personal spiritual companionship and retreats, the relentless struggle for peace and justice, in what they write and teach and do (which is often in courageous resistance to oppressive movements both in the Church and in the world) and in the practical support of asylum seekers and all who are dispossessed or marginalized.

The Ignatian tradition, practised and taught faithfully and imaginatively by the most inspired and creative of today's Jesuits and those who work alongside them, has become a powerful catalyst for an authentic renewal of lived Christianity in our times. It is a 'feet-on-the-ground' approach to all that it might mean to live our own lives as 'companions of Christ'.

2

Down to Earth with God

The fish and the ocean

Anthony de Mello tells a tale of a fish who spent all its life searching for that mystery that goes by the name 'ocean'. 'What is "ocean"?' it kept on asking all those it met. 'I have looked everywhere, spent all my life swimming in every possible direction, and still I don't know what "ocean" is. Do you know what?' it concluded finally. 'I don't think I believe in this thing called "ocean". How should I believe in something I've never seen, and no-one can describe for me?'

And this reminds me, in turn, of a comment made in the film *City of Angels*, in which an angel called Seth enters into a love relationship with a woman on earth. She questions the reality of what she is feeling for this man who is half there and half not, occasionally palpable to her but mainly invisible. Seth listens quietly to her struggles to believe, and then makes his response: 'Some things are true whether you believe in them or not.'

I can feel with the fish. And I can feel with the woman who is so deeply loved by a being beyond her ability to imagine, let alone to relate to. When I am drifting aimlessly through life, or when I am feeling driven by all the demands it makes upon me, I feel like the fish. I feel I have to find my own way, do my own thing, justify my existence in some way. I dart about in the waters of life, deluding myself into thinking it is all down to me – to make a living, to stay afloat, and – yes – to pray! Then in my darker moments I thrash around looking for 'God', and feel tempted to wonder whether the whole thing is just a figment of my imagination. It is then that I need to read that de Mello story, and remember that the One I am seeking is actually in everything, whatever name I give to that One, and the name we mainly give is 'God'. God is what gives me life in the first place and what keeps me alive. God is what gives me meaning. God is my context for being and my reason for being, and it is actually all down to God, not me. Even when I think I am praying, it is actually 'God' (whatever and whoever we mean by that) who is breathing God's breath through me and bringing my soul to life. Oh, and by the way, de Mello was a Jesuit, and therefore very familiar with the Ignatian invitation to 'find God in all things', except that he would surely have added the advice to 'find all things in God'.

And I can feel with Seth's beloved too. She knows that her life is being touched and shaped by an invisible presence that she knows must be angelic, but her mind tells her that such things cannot be. She is a scientist. How is she supposed to believe in angels? But it doesn't matter. What is true is true, and it doesn't need the rubber stamp of our creeds to make it so. That gives me a strange kind of reassurance – not to make myself believe in a set of facts because I have to recite them in order to be baptized or confirmed – but a reassurance that this whole thing is way beyond my mind's grasp, but nevertheless I can trust my lived experience of its effects on me.

I think Ignatius would have warmed to both of those stories, because he embarked on his own spiritual journey trusting only in his experience of how this immense and loving power that we call God (though others might use a different name) had brought him to a new dimension of life. He encourages us to engage with the Christ-story in the same spirit – allowing it to work its deep transformation within us, rather than learning the facts as if for an exam.

Inhabitants of eternity

In his book *Anam Cara*, John O'Donohue suggests that 'the human person is a threshold where many infinities meet'. One implication of this is that wherever and whoever God is for us, we will, and can only meet this God where we are, in our embodied living, on our planet earth, in the living universe that enfolds our planet, and in the everyday world where we live and move and have our being. If we don't meet God in the everyday, we won't meet God at all, just as the only place where the fish can encounter the ocean is in the very spot where it swims.

It is hard to look upon our – mainly mundane – everyday experience as the place, and the only place where we will encounter the mystery we call God. It just seems so unlikely. So we search out the mountain-tops and great temples and cathedrals instead, and we put God into this special slot – something for Sundays. The weekdays are really no fit place for God to tread, we can slip into thinking. We make a clear distinction in our minds, at least in most of the Western world, between 'sacred' and 'secular', the 'divine' and the 'human'. It is hard to *trust* our experience as a place of encounter with God. But not everyone feels like this. The Jesuit poet Gerard Manley Hopkins, for example, declares with passionate exuberance that

> The world is charged with the grandeur of God.
> It will flame out, like shining from shook foil.
>
> ('God's Grandeur')

It might be interesting to do just that – to get out the roll of baking foil from the kitchen and shake it out. Listen to the shimmering, quivering sound it makes as it cascades to the floor. But we daren't unroll God like that. We prefer to keep God safely rolled up in the kitchen drawer. We might never get God back in God's proper place, under our control, if we once let God unfurl Godself all over our everyday life.

But of course God doesn't need our permission to quiver and shimmer through our experience. Such shimmering is an ever-present reality – as constantly present to us as the ocean is to the fish, and true, whether we believe it or not. All that is needed to 'make it incarnate' is 'eyes to see and ears to hear': *our* eyes, and *our* ears. In their book *The Universe Story*, Brian Swimme and Thomas Berry explore the unfolding of Godself through the eons of evolution in terms of a conversation, reflecting an unbreakable communion: 'The universe was a dramatic reality, filled with powers and voices constituting the Great Conversation that humans participated in through daily and seasonal rituals as well as through rituals associated with birth, maturity and death' (p. 153). To this one might add, 'and through the growing awareness of the value of every moment, every meeting, every happenstance of their lived experience every day'. For every moment is a moment in which we can either encounter the divine, or miss the opportunity. One of the great gifts of Ignatian spirituality is the signpost that directs our gaze to what is actually happening in the here and now, and bears the words: 'Look *here*!'

Finding God in all things . . .

So how do we come to this kind of heightened awareness? How do we turn the vague desire to 'find God in all things' into a living reality with the power to renew and revitalize us moment by moment?

Ignatius suggests a very simple but very powerful tool that is often called 'The Review of the Day' (also sometimes referred to by its older name, The Examen). If you think you can't pray, or if you feel you never have the time or space for prayer, this simple routine might be worth its weight in gold. All that is required is a short period once a day, at a time that feels right for you, during which you simply look back over what has been going on in and around you during the preceding 24 hours. The rest of this chapter will offer some suggestions about what you might be looking out for.

This kind of prayer is not for focusing on what *you* have been getting wrong, or even getting right, through the day, but where *God* has felt real and alive to you. It is a question of focus – like Inigo's daydreams that we shared in Chapter 1, remembering that the *self-focused* dreams led nowhere, and left him feeling desolate, while the *God-focused* dreams inspired him and empowered him into new levels of commitment and new horizons of vision. It is a time of relaxed awareness, simply noticing, without any judgement of yourself or anyone else, what memories surface of the day's events and encounters, how you feel about them, and what God is revealing about Godself, and about you and your relationship with God and with the rest of God's creation, through these reactions and responses. Don't try to do a postmortem on every incident and conversation, but simply notice and become aware of any specific moments that your memory sends up to your conscious mind, trusting that these prompts are coming from God, who is present and active deep in your own psyche, just as in every other created space.

There is a story of how, at the beginning of time, God decided to hide in the created universe, and God summoned three angels to advise on a suitable hiding-place. The first angel suggested that God might hide in the depths of the earth. 'A good idea,' said God. 'I will indeed hide myself in the earth, but it won't be long before they learn to mine the earth, and they will surely find me too easily. Where else can I hide?' The second angel suggested the moon as a hiding-place. 'An excellent idea,' said God. 'I will indeed hide myself in the expanses of space and the sun and moon and stars, but it won't be long before they discover how to explore space, and they will find me too soon. Where else can I hide?' So the third angel hit on a very original idea: 'Why don't you hide yourself in their own hearts? They'll never think to look for you there!' And so God did all three of those things. God hid in the earth and all that it contains. God hid in the vastness of interstellar space. And God hid in the innermost heart of every creature. And why did God hide at all? Because it is in our *search* for the God who says 'I am who I am', that we do our growing and becoming, and discovering who *we* truly and eternally are.

The Review prayer searches for God in these places too. It invites us to notice God in the created world and in all that happens to us and through us. And then it invites us to go into our own hearts, and to listen there in silence to the still murmurings of God, showing us gently what in our experience is leading us closer to God and our own deepest truth, and what is tending to draw us away from that true centre.

With this intention, therefore, and this desire to seek God's presence in the lived events of our day, let's look now at some of the possibilities.

God in the narrative of every day

What has been going on in your world today? Maybe there was a moment when you felt really alive – maybe someone showed their love or concern for you, a child took hold of your hand with an absolute trust, a letter arrived that gave you encouragement or affirmation, a passing stranger smiled or acknowledged you as a person who matters, someone walked the extra mile with you when they could have taken the short cut home. These were incidents when the God of love was revealing Godself in and through the choices and actions of other human beings.

However, the day may have brought its challenges. Maybe something went wrong at work, and you were criticized. Maybe someone pressed you for a decision on something you were prevaricating over. Maybe that awful neighbour rang your door bell, and there was nowhere to hide from her demands. Maybe your child or partner provoked you and you had to choose whether to react in anger or with forbearance. All these are ways in which God says, 'Life isn't easy – how are you going to choose to react?'

Or perhaps your day was a non-starter. Nothing happened. Nobody came near you. The children didn't phone, the friend you expected didn't turn up, there was nothing on TV. Where is God in the disappointments and disillusionments of our everyday living? I hope we will discover some answers to this kind of question as we move on in our exploration of Ignatian spirituality. For now, just hold it right there, registering how you are really feeling about your day, and trusting God to receive your feelings just as they are.

God in the created universe

When the day gets the better of me and I am feeling drained of energy and enthusiasm, one quick cure can be to take a walk down the garden or to the park. For one thing, the exercise in itself helps to change my focus from how fed-up I am feeling to that huge world of otherness beyond my own ego-world. Even the slightest shift of focus like this can open my heart to the gentle movements of God's spirit. Once among the trees, I can reconnect to creation as the place where I too live and move and have my being. The sap that rises through the trees and the flowers and the grass is energized by the same life that keeps the blood coursing through my veins. All that lives and grows has deep, hidden roots that draw sustenance from the rich dark soil, and I am part of this same world. I have roots too, and the garden reminds me to trust them. Just to stand still in a world that is all about rootedness, growth, seasonal dying and new life is to realize that we too belong to this same world.

As you look back over the day, it may be helpful just to recall anything in the created world that has touched your life today – the morning birdsong, fresh buds in springtime, the gentle turning of a leaf from green to gold, a full moon, a turbulent cloudscape, the affection of your pet. You may realize that in fact you have rushed through the day without even noticing the natural world, and certainly without pausing to smell the roses. If so, don't judge yourself, but make the choice for a deeper awareness tomorrow, and a conscious decision to take time – however briefly – to connect to the created world.

God in our own story and the world's story

Many of us came into the world as inheritors of the 'mechanistic universe' theory. Life, it was thought for several centuries preceding our own, was like a huge machine that God had once kick-started, and then left to its own devices.

If we could just understand how every part worked, we would understand the secret of life. Now, in all the main branches of science, people are discovering a very different story. Life, we are beginning to realize, is an unfolding process, rather than a fixed system of interlocking but largely autonomous parts. It is an unfolding process in which every molecule is interconnected with, and affected by, every other molecule. It has evolved from what the physicists call a 'singularity' by a mind-blowing series of progressions and setbacks, including many near-extinctions; and it is by no means complete.

Discovering God in this story is one of the most exciting challenges of our century, but it also helps to remind us that our own personal story is an essential thread in the weaving of the universe story. Anyone embarking on a spiritual journey based on the Ignatian way would certainly be encouraged to spend some time reflecting on their own sacred story, and where God has been in it for them.

You might like to pause to consider the trail that your own life is tracing. Just remember in a spirit of prayerful awareness the events, relationships and developments that you feel, in hindsight, have formed you most significantly into who you are today.

Remember the people who have helped to shape your personality. If you were compiling a small photo album to take with you to a desert island, whose pictures would you include? And why? What significant incidents would you want to record? Which relationships have become part of who you are? How has your journey with God evolved, since that moment, some nine months before your birth, when you were just a single fertilized cell? What do you want especially to thank God for? Is there anything you are angry about? If so, tell God how you are really feeling. It may be the very thing God is wanting to address with you.

You may discover, as you recall the course your life has taken, that the points of greatest spiritual growth coincided not with the high points, in human terms, but with the times of failure, betrayal, disappointment or even despair. Certainly this was true for Ignatius. It was in the pain and humiliation of defeat and incapacity that he discovered his great desire for God, and in the depths of darkness he experienced in Manresa that the *Spiritual Exercises* were gestating.

God in each other

One thing that is taught in all spiritual traditions is that if we don't find God in our neighbour, we won't find God at all. This is easy to affirm on Sunday morning in a peaceful parish church. It takes on different colours altogether on Monday morning in the traffic queues, the workplace, the supermarket, the school run, the hospital ward or the social security office. The neighbour we say we want to love as we love ourselves becomes, from Monday to Saturday, our rival in the rat-race for survival and for a bigger slice of life's cake.

I discovered, one year in retreat, that I needed some prescription lenses. I needed a pair of bifocal specs, that would allow me to keep on living my ordinary life in a decent kind of a way, without falling down too many potholes, but that at the same time would enable me to look into the faces of the people around me – especially those I live and work with – and see the presence of God in their eyes.

One of the hardest challenges we face as human beings is not the heroics of martyrdom at all, but the everyday hurdle of getting along with those who push and jostle all around us. We could, perhaps, cheerfully sell up and give half our gains to the starving poor. The real problem is to stay put and get on with the guy next door.

Perhaps, therefore, the Review prayer could do well to include some moments of reflection on 'who was my neighbour today?' Have you caught a glimpse of God in another human face today? Perhaps it was in the eyes of a homeless teenager, or an overworked cashier at a supermarket checkout. Perhaps a baby looked into your eyes and you saw the world anew in her glance. Was God there when an elderly relative looked at you mutely, hoping for five minutes of your attention? Or when your child wanted you to listen to his new CD? Eternity is made up of a million moments of possibility like these. Don't judge yourself when you miss a few, or even most of them. There will be many more tomorrow, and in each human face you look into with love, you will see a reflection of God's love shining back.

God in beauty, truth, compassion and integrity

I remember singing the hymn at school: 'God is good! God is truth! God is beauty! Praise him!' At the time, goodness, truth and beauty were just abstract concepts, and the admonition to 'praise him!' felt more like a threat than an invitation. 'Praise him, or else!' Now, however, I find that these qualities I once found so meaningless at a personal level can become gateways into prayer. No one can name or describe God. At best we can only pick up on one or other of the characteristics we feel, instinctively, in all spiritual traditions, that God must possess. Why do we feel this? Surely, because these are qualities we value universally in the human being, and we intuit that if they are in us, the creatures, they must surely be present in their completeness, in the source of our life, the creator. We sense that what we value so highly in its imperfect form in ourselves, must have its deep source and perfect fulfilment in God.

The Ignatian emphasis on an earthed spirituality has helped me to move beyond regarding these qualities as something abstract and forever out of reach – my own truth and integrity are terribly flawed and selective, my compassion is always patchy and sometimes non-existent, and I am certainly not a thing of beauty. But I can find these qualities around me. They are there in obvious ways – in the beauty of art, the truth of literature, the compassion of the caring professions – but they are also there in more hidden guises. For example, I may discover that the person who criticizes me is also one who sees the truth of things more clearly than I do, and whom I would do well to listen to. He may be speaking God's truth to me. The woman who has been so badly hurt that I simply don't know what to say to her, may be such a carrier of compassion for others who are hurting that I have everything to learn from her. The child with the marred body or the damaged mind may be shining inwardly with God's beauty, if I have the courage to approach more closely and embrace what I find.

God in the apparent absence of God

But what about all those times, and those areas of our lives, that feel as though God has never been anywhere near them? Accustomed as we are to view our relationship with God as that between a judge and a penitent, we can so very easily produce a catalogue of failures to present to God in prayer. Ignatius himself needed three full days to make his confession at Montserrat, and even then he couldn't leave well alone and accept the fact of his forgiveness. He continued to battle with scruples through the long dark months in Manresa. So if, at the end of the day, we find there is nothing much to report or to notice except our own shortcomings, we may slip into thinking that God hasn't been in our day at all – or indeed that God has made only fleeting visits in our life generally.

Yet the fact remains that, if we believe the Christian gospel, Jesus himself was making that crucial breakthrough, past the cross and all it represents, into something we can't imagine, but that he called 'life in all its fullness', at precisely the point when he was utterly empty, lonely and racked by the sense that he had been abandoned even by God. Might it not be the case, therefore, that when we ourselves feel that God is a million miles away, and completely absent from our day-to-day struggling, that this is precisely the place where God is most active?

This doesn't just have to remain a pious hope. As we noticed earlier in this chapter, it often happens that our most significant spiritual growth occurs not when we are riding on the crest of a wave, but when we are right down there in the trough, though we will usually only see the evidence of this growth with the benefit of hindsight. Creation tells us the same story. The most profound growth almost always happens in the darkness. Bulbs and seeds grow in the darkness of the earth. Babies grow in the darkness of the womb. The process of growth is an invisible one. The nourishment that fosters growth comes in the darkness and has to be received by faith.

> Can you look back and notice this process at work in previous phases of your life? If so, name these phases to yourself, and reflect back on how they were, and what new growth emerged out of them. Can you trust the process to be at work in whatever may lie ahead? You might let these questions simply hover gently in your prayer, without trying to force any answers.

In all that gives us life

God is the God of life. We have reflected on some of the ways in which that all-pervading life touches our own consciousness and how we might build in this kind of awareness into our daily living, in some form of Awareness Prayer, or Review of the Day. The very many ways in which God reveals Godself in our everyday lives and the world around us might be summarized simply like this:

> What has given me life today? What has made me feel more alive, more human? These questions might then lead us on to reflect: In what ways have I been a source of life, hope, encouragement, trust or love to other people and to the rest of creation? For any ways in which I have failed, and for the many opportunities I will have missed, I confidently beg God's forgiveness and entrust tomorrow to God's care and keeping.

In the book of Exodus 33.23, God says: 'You will see my back, but my face will not be seen.'

'God's back' may not sound very visionary or inspiring, thus transcribed into our prosaic language and imagery. But think about it! Everywhere we look, in every nook and cranny of creation, ourselves included, we see the traces of where God has passed! We see a universe that bears the imprint of this mystery and this wisdom in every molecule. What a pity if we were to be so obsessed with seeing 'God's face' – in trying to define and dissect a mystery that lies forever beyond us – that we were to miss this overwhelming evidence of a Presence that will always be moving on, leading us forward, before we could ever possibly catch up with it. Whatever gives life – the amazing structures of our bodies, the subtle nuances of our thinking minds, the gentle movements of love that warm our hearts – these in all their infinite variety of manifestations continue to give us life, as the ocean holds the fish in being. *Ubi vita, ibi Deus est.* Where there is life, there is God.

3

Living True

The invisible thread

There is a haunting folk story about a little girl who strayed one day into a big castle. After exploring the castle for a long time she discovered her old granny, hidden away in a garret, spinning golden thread. A joyful reunion followed, and the old granny gave the child a gold ring. 'This ring', she explained, 'is attached by a golden thread to this golden ball here in my garret. I hold the golden ball in my hands and in my heart, and as long as you hold the ring that connects you to me by this golden thread, you will never be lost.'

The child was delighted with the ring, but at the same time dismayed: the golden thread that joined it to her granny's golden ball was invisible! She went back into the world both full of hope and full of doubt, holding her ring close, but never really knowing for sure whether the golden thread was still in place or not.

This story speaks to me. A spiritual journey – especially a Christian journey – can feel a lot like that. God, we believe, holds the core of our being, like that golden ball in the loving granny's hands, and we ourselves hold at least a token of the eternal connection that links the God within us for ever with the God beyond us. That 'token' may mean different things for different people. For some it may be the 'ring' of baptism, and of being sacramentally received into

God's family through the Church. For others it may be personal experience alone that assures them that there is something of God within them, regardless of whether they are formally members of any church. Whatever form it takes for us, we have our own 'gold ring' that reminds us that we are connected to the source of all being. But the thread that connects us is, for most of the time, invisible! So, for us as for that little girl, it is likely to be a case of proceeding both in hope and in doubt, confident and hesitant, assured of 'the Way', but at the same time blind and stumbling.

When I first came across this story I knew that I had discovered at least one answer to the question that was once put to Peter: 'Who do you say that I am?' Who is Jesus for me? Who is Jesus for you? The credal declarations don't answer this question adequately for me any more. But, for now at least, the little girl with her invisible thread *does*. This man, Jesus of Nazareth, is the one who, for me, makes the invisible thread visible. He makes the eternal connection between the core of our own being and the source of all being into something we can see and hear, relate to and learn from, love and follow.

It is easy to say and write things like this, but what does it mean in practice? Ignatian spirituality is a very practical way of living a life of Christian discipleship, so we can justifiably look to it for some useful tools that may work for us in the nitty-gritty of daily life. We believe, as Christians, that Jesus is a man whose life shows us what it means to be perfectly attuned to God and to live true to that inner alignment. But how, exactly, are we to see and hear him, relate to him, learn from him, love and follow him?

Ignatius was learning precisely this in the despondency of Manresa, and the central focus of his *Spiritual Exercises* is the making of a personal journey through the Gospel narratives that tell us what kind of a man this Jesus was, how he lived, what his attitudes and values were about, and how he connected heaven and earth in ways that impacted those around him with a fresh and stunning authenticity. That was two thousand years ago. Does it work for us today? Can the spirit of this man still energize and transform in the way he clearly did when he walked the streets of Jerusalem and the hillsides of Galilee? The Ignatian *Exercises* give us an opportunity and an invitation to find out – to discover for ourselves whether this gospel has the power we are told it has. They can be a key that turns rote religion into a living spirituality.

To earth from heaven?

Every Christmas we sing it, for sure, and probably many times in between: 'God came down to earth from heaven.' I never used to question it, but I am becoming increasingly uncomfortable with an image that suggests that 'God' is somehow eternally 'up there', and, at a particular moment in human history, decided to 'come down'.

Yet the fact of the incarnation is real and powerful, challenging us and at the same time reassuring us, that whatever is going on in our lives, God is somehow in it with us. And the gospel journey into which Ignatius invites us begins with a meditation on the incarnation. This can be the first challenge to move beyond the formulations of creed and doctrine, towards a living spirituality that makes a real difference to how we live and relate to each other today in the twenty-first century.

What might it mean for us today to reflect on this decisive moment when God 'came down to earth'?

As I write, the first daffodils are coming into bloom. For weeks now the tight green shoots and buds have been visible. Then, during the last few days of warm sunshine, those tight buds have swollen with their golden pregnancy, and now, one after another, they are coming to birth. We could say the daffodils have come again. But, of course, the daffodils were always there, through the long cold winter, and they will still be there when these April blossoms have died away again. The daffodils are a permanent presence in the earth. And so, surely, is God a permanent presence in God's creation, and not some visiting alien who 'landed' for thirty years, two millennia ago.

Nevertheless, the daffodils *reveal* themselves in a special, dramatic and beautiful way, during a few short weeks in springtime. Just so, I am convinced, did God reveal Godself in a special way at a particular time in our human story. God revealed Godself when the time was right, just as the daffodils come to bloom when the conditions are just right. Their, and God's, self-revelation is a sign that a new phase of growth is beginning. The daffodils' appearance heralds the start of spring. God's appearance, in the life of Jesus of Nazareth, heralds a whole new stage of the growth in loving consciousness of the inhabitants of planet Earth.

For reasons we may never understand, around two thousand years ago we reached a point in our evolution that marked a certain readiness for a quantum leap forward in our awareness of what it means to be human. Jesus, for me, is the one who calls us, and empowers us, to make that quantum leap – not rejecting all that went before, but building upon it and transforming it. To embrace this new covenant is not just another way of 'doing religion'. It is, I would suggest, the evolutionary challenge of our age.

The message of the gospel is not so much a matter of historical fact or even of vague memories. It is something immediate and *now*. When I encounter the Jesus of the Gospels, in my own prayer and reflection on the scriptures, I meet someone who isn't asking me to subscribe to a belief system but is challenging me to embrace a whole new way of being human. In Jesus I meet, not so much the God who 'comes down' for a visit, but the God who 'comes up', emerging out of the very same earth of which we ourselves are made. God, whether we are aware of God or not, is totally and eternally present in the very ground of our being – the ground of being in each creature, and the ground of being of all creation. This God is the one who 'comes up', in a special way, when the conditions are right. This was the case, it appears, two thousand years ago, in the story of humankind. And for each one of us, there will also be a moment (or maybe many such moments) when the conditions are right and God reveals Godself in a special kind of way. Both collectively, and individually, this self-revelation of God heralds new growth for God's creation.

The daffodils herald the coming of the season when everything in the garden will come to its own flowering and fruitfulness. When God emerges from the earth, in the body, mind and soul of a baby born to an ordinary girl in the Middle East, a wake-up call quivers through all creation. A new age is dawning, and for Christians Jesus is its trailblazer. He is, in his own words, 'the Way' from this moment on. He is also 'Truth' and 'Life'. Jesus described himself as the first of many brothers and sisters. Once the first daffodil bud has opened to the springtime, hundreds more follow in quick succession. 'I tell you,' Jesus says, 'some here will still be alive to see the first manifestations of this new kingdom, this new stage of human-being coming to birth on planet Earth.'

One of my personal debts to Ignatian spirituality is that it has given me tools with which to discover for myself how I too can participate in this new way of being human, under Jesus' tutelage, learning, day by day, to live true to the best in my humanity, by following and learning from one who embodies True Life for all humanity. We will explore some of these tools in the remainder of this book.

The axis of life

Another picture that I carry around in my mind and imagination is that of all creation spinning around a vast
invisible axis that holds it in being, keeping every particle of
creation in right relationship with every other particle. This
is just an image – and all our mental images are necessarily
partial and can even be misleading, especially when they are
suggesting themselves as images of God. Even so, this image
of God as the axis that holds everything in being is one I
find helpful.

It becomes even more helpful if I think of that axis as
running not just through the heart of all creation, but also
through my own heart. If I could only live true to the very
best in me, then my whole life would spin about this axis in
balance and in right relationship. I hardly need to add that
this is almost never the case. Whatever the 'Fall' means, one
of the consequences of it is that we have certainly lost that
relational balance within ourselves, with those around us,
and with the wider creation. We are no longer 'running
true' to this invisible axis, whom we might name 'God'. We
have lost sight of the thread that connects us to granny's
golden ball. We are living in a world that is tragically dis-
located. We are both implicated in, and affected by, every
aspect of that trauma.

The good news is that we have, in Jesus of Nazareth, a
model of what it means to live completely true to that 'axis
of life'. Jesus lived a life that was not off-key and out of
balance as ours are. He allowed the true axis to determine
all his actions and relationships. He lived out for us the
possibility that we too could be brought back into this
perfect balance and alignment with God. He taught us that,
to the extent that we choose to allow this to happen in us,
we will be furthering the 'coming of the Kingdom of God',
the new age of heightened loving awareness that will carry

all creation forward towards entirely new levels of consciousness that we, in our present condition, cannot even
begin to imagine.

Yet Jesus is more than just a model. He lived the True
Life in his earthly ministry, but he also paid the price for
living true. In a world riddled with falsehood, deception
and self-deception, the one who lives true will not be
tolerated. Those he came to call put him to death. The cross
thus becomes the 'narrow gate' through which we must
expect to have to pass, each in our own way, if we are
serious about seeking to live true to the True Life that Jesus
embodies and makes visible and real. What happens
beyond that narrow gate of Calvary is the springtime that
Jesus' coming to birth proclaimed. We do well not to try to
be too specific about what exactly that means, any more
than an unborn child should speculate on the nature of life
beyond the womb.

The carpenter's workshop

Our daughter is a medical student. Her training consists
mainly of so-called 'clinical rotations'. This means that she
spends several weeks at a time working alongside the medical teams in different specialities. Her task is to observe, to
learn, and then to practise. She is given an opportunity to
stand beside those who are already skilled in their profession, to learn those skills 'on the job', and to put them into
practice in a carefully supervised situation. This whole learning process is reminiscent of the traditional apprenticeships
that young people would undergo. The idea was to learn by
observing the master craftsman at work, and by practising
the skills for oneself, until proficiency was attained.

Perhaps it is no coincidence that Jesus of Nazareth spent
his formative years in a workshop, at the bench of a crafts-

man. Jesus was apprentice-trained, in the carpentry profession. He learned from his father Joseph, first by watching, and then by carrying out the tasks himself. But, of course, that is not how we remember Nazareth's most famous son . . . is it? Well, ironically, it is this 'apprenticeship' image that shapes a major component of the *Spiritual Exercises*. Ignatius invites us to make an apprentice journey, in the same kind of way as Jesus learned carpentry, and as our daughter is learning to be a doctor. We are urged to follow the master craftsman, to watch him at work, to learn everything he has to show us about how to be truly human in all of life's complex situations, and then to go out and practise what we have learned, for the benefit of all creation. It is really as simple as that – and as hard!

It is simple because we only have to copy what we see in Jesus, the one who lives true to the divine axis of life and love. It is hard because we constantly encounter distractions that pull us off course, and we are continually tempted to believe that we can do things so much better our own way. We are not the most biddable of apprentices. At our worst, we are every teacher's nightmare.

So how do we begin to make such a journey, learning, quite literally, at the feet of this man Jesus? Ignatius takes us to the heart of the matter, which is to be found in the Gospel accounts of Jesus' life and ministry. And he urges us to get right in there, as if we were personally present to the events that are described. It doesn't matter that we don't know what first-century Galilee was really like. It doesn't matter whether the historical details recorded by the Gospel writers are literally precise. We are dealing here with the Jewish tradition of *midrash* – the power of story that communicates deep truth, and what matters is what these events *mean* for us personally in twenty-first-century life. It matters how we respond in a personal way to what the teacher reveals.

When I attend a 'workshop', I do so with some trepidation. There is a large part of me that would much prefer to listen to a lecture, maybe take notes, and then file the notes and the insights away in some compartment of my brain, in case they ever come in useful. I tend to cringe when the workshop leader suggests active participation! And I know, from experience as a rather reluctant workshop leader, that I am not alone in my bashfulness! But Jesus is a practical man. He doesn't give lectures – he offers workshops. And these are very hands-on affairs. Nor are they about things as they were two thousand years ago. They are contemporary workshops. He invites us to learn alongside him in this very earthed and relevant way. Not to get a set of notes to file away. Not to pass an exam. But to become more and more infused and *enthused* by the values and attitudes of this man who lived in such true and close alignment with the core of all being, that people called him the Son of God (though he himself preferred the name Son of Man, which I am told means 'an ordinary guy').

Just pause for a moment to reflect on this invitation. Let Jesus approach you and invite you, by name, to follow him as his apprentice. The call to 'follow me' may be as simple as this – not an impossible challenge to drop everything you ever wanted and do something radically different, but rather to become more aware of the things you are actually doing in your life, and to see them, and maybe do them (or even stop doing them!) in a radically different way. If you are willing to follow, he will take you with him into the various situations and events that he encountered himself during his earthly life. He will encourage you simply to be there, watching what happens, observing his own reactions and the attitudes and values they reveal. He is a patient teacher. He will wait for as long as it takes for you to assimilate something of his own way of living true. He won't rush you, but he will be hoping that you will be beginning to put into practice what you are learning.

At the beginning of this chapter we reflected on the possibility that Jesus of Nazareth is a man who makes visible and tangible the invisible thread connecting the core of our own being to the core of all being, in God. The Gospels provide us with the key to unlock the secrets of this man's life and ministry, and, indeed, to become empowered ourselves to 'go and do likewise'.

There are several tried and tested ways of entering the Gospels personally. They are not original to Ignatius, but they are methods he strongly endorses. Three methods in particular are suggested below to help you to enter deeply into the Gospel stories and find your own story in the midst of them. Try them for yourself, and see what works for you.

Imaginative meditation

Choose any incident from the Gospels that especially appeals to you. Relax, maybe close your eyes, and let your imagination visualize the scene. Take in all the details, as they present themselves to your inner senses: the sights, sounds and smells; the atmosphere; the people present; and your own place in it all. Let the scene be whatever your imagination suggests – don't try to reconstruct the way you think Palestine might have looked.

Now notice where you find *yourself* in this scene. Perhaps in the centre of the action? Perhaps a detached bystander? Perhaps receiving Jesus' personal healing or forgiveness, or perhaps being too afraid to go anywhere near him? Maybe actively assisting him, or standing on the edge of the crowd, not wanting to get involved? Don't make any judgements about what your scene brings up for you. Just notice. Now try taking the prayer further. Is there anything you want to say to Jesus? Anything you feel you want to do? And, most crucially, where and how do you notice any personal connections between the scene you are praying and your own lived experience, your personal circumstances, situations and relationships? Take anything you discover into prayer, perhaps talking to Jesus about it.

If you found yourself reluctant to enter the scene, reflect prayerfully (but non-judgementally) on why this might be so. Notice especially any strong feelings or reactions, either positive or negative, that are coming up for you, and take these into a process of *deepening down* (see below).

Saturation prayer

Another way to immerse ourselves in the Gospel stories is in the ancient form of scriptural prayer known as *lectio divina*. This form of prayer goes right back to the times when very few people could read. In the monasteries, therefore, one monk would read extracts from the Gospel, or other scripture, and keep on repeating the text, slowly and reflectively, several times over. The other monks would listen carefully, until a particular phrase or image 'came alive' for them in a personal way, attracting their attention especially. Once a monk had 'caught his fish' for the day, he would go off to his cell and chew it over and over, extracting all its meaning and power for him, letting it settle deeply into his mind and heart, where he trusted that it would be working its invisible transformation.

This form of prayer lends itself very readily to today's busy world too. Try reading a short extract, maybe in the morning before the day gets under way, and noticing any part of it – a phrase, a picture it evokes, or an idea it sparks. Then carry your nugget of gold with you through the day, getting it out again whenever you think of it, chewing it over, almost unconsciously, as the day goes on. If you don't know where to start, there are several daily reading booklets, offering a suggested scriptural passage each day, with some commentary. Most Christian bookshops will stock a selection of these. Otherwise, simply follow your nose – maybe choosing one of the Gospels, and reading it through a bit at a time, day by day. If you are used to a set lectionary, you might like to use the official daily readings as a starting point.

But the reading *is* only the starting point. The depth of the exercise lies in your connecting with whatever speaks to you personally, and then letting that phrase or image sink deep into your being, trusting that God will be working transformatively in your life through this channel.

Deepening down

These two ways of praying with scripture are tried and tested, and they both have the power to touch into the deeper reaches of your psyche. So what happens if you notice some personal connection, finding yourself somehow involved in a Gospel scene (in ways that may have taken you by surprise), or feeling attracted to a particular phrase or image in the text?

Just to notice these moments of connection can be the beginning of deeper prayer. What you do with the connection you have noticed is, of course, up to you, but a very good way to take the prayer further is to use what Ignatius calls the prayer of *repetition*. This doesn't mean repeating the whole process. It means noticing the particular part of the prayer or meditation that gave rise to a strong reaction. Perhaps you felt very close to Jesus, or very far away, in an imaginative meditation, and something urges you to get to the root of your reaction. Perhaps a phrase came alive for you, but you are not yet sure exactly why, or what hidden treasure it still holds for you. At this point it can be extremely helpful to go back to that point of connectedness, and go deeper, focusing your meditation on that particular spot, and noticing what it yields. Sometimes this kind of deepening prayer can work down into your heart like a life-giving spiral, opening up parts of your being that God is seeking to heal or inspire, or enliven in some new way.

In all of these forms of prayer, you will have noticed that your own feelings and reactions play an important part. This may surprise you. Often our religious education teaches us to set aside our own feelings. Ignatius insists, on the contrary, that our feelings can be indicators of what is happening in the roots of our being, and can guide us to those parts of our life that especially need God's touch right now. We will explore this matter of moods and feelings more fully in the next chapter.

Putting it into practice

These three methods of scriptural prayer are among the tools we find in the workshop. They help us to come close to the Master as he works. Jesus is the Master of the True Life, and these tools help us to observe him as he teaches and heals, challenges, confronts and consoles. The purpose of such prayer is to learn from the Master – not so much the techniques (as we might learn a craft), but the attitudes and values he displays. It gives us an opportunity to discover, for example:

- How Jesus deals with those who are on the margins of society
- How he reacts to those whose lives are 'out of order'
- How he responds to hypocrisy
- How he handles the tensions with religious and secular authorities

- How he relates to the suffering of others, and to his own sufferings
- How he remains in right relationship with the Father
- What matters to him, and what is unimportant
- What makes him tick

In short, it invites us into personal friendship and companionship with the one who, above all, lived *true*. If we really desire to live our own lives along this true axis, what better way to learn?

But of course, to learn is one thing, to practise is another. I remember our daughter's first encounters with real patients. She had learned the procedures in the lecture room, and practised them on other students. Now it was time to use her embryonic skills on those who were in need of help. We too are called to put into practice the values and attitudes we are learning as apprentices to the Master of the True Life. This sounds daunting, but there are some simple guidelines that might help us as we venture forth:

- In every situation that arises, we can ask: What would Jesus do in this situation?
- If this isn't obvious, we can ask: What is the more loving thing to do next? What action, or reaction, is more likely to lead to an increase of hope, trust and love in the world?

We may be facing a life-changing challenge, or a trivial incident. The same principles apply. From all we are learning from our prayerful immersion in the values of the Gospel, what do we feel about how Jesus would respond? We will get it wrong, of course. We may completely neglect to ask the question, when push comes to shove. Or we may ask the question, recognize the more Christ-like course, but still do the opposite! We are learners. As seekers of the True

Life, we all need a huge L-plate on our backs. God isn't going to harangue us over every failure. Rather, like a good parent or teacher, God is going to help us to learn from our mistakes, and one excellent way to do some remedial work is in the Review prayer that we considered in Chapter 2.

From workshop to workplace

There is no graduation ceremony! That is not what it is about. When it comes to the quest to live true, we go on learning all our lives. We remain disciples – ones who learn – because there is always more to learn. Every new situation, encounter and relationship brings new challenges, and demands new ways of asking: What is the more loving, the more Christ-like thing to do here?

Nevertheless, the pattern of the Gospels reveals that the disciples also become apostles. They remain 'those who are learning' but they also become 'those who are sent out'. Our genuine desire to live our own lives by the values of Jesus of Nazareth will percolate through every aspect of our daily living, and have its effect through all we do and say, at home, at work, at leisure, in sickness and in health, in well-being and in destitution.

Jesus went about the world being Christ, touching those around him with God's love. To be a disciple is to learn from him how this is done. To be an apostle is to go out and do it ourselves, empowered by the energy we call the Holy Spirit.

4

First Principles, Firm Foundations

Remember Seth – the angel who reminds us that 'some things are true whether you believe them or not'? Well, unfortunately, the converse is also true. Some things are not true, however firmly you believe them. Some things are illusions. In fact a great deal of what we cling to so fiercely, trusting it to be so solid, is an illusion. And it can be much, much easier to believe in, and to act upon, our illusions than to listen to, and act upon, the truth.

It begins with our own bodies. We seem, and feel, solid enough, yet molecular biologists tell us that we are actually made up of over 99 per cent empty space. The reality is that we are held together by a combination of forces of which we are wholly unconscious, and which most of us wouldn't begin to understand. And those same forces, so we are beginning to discover, are guided by a wisdom quite incomprehensible to our own minds, which organizes almost nothing into the amazing complexities of life on this planet. Truly, what you see is a mere fraction of what you get. What appears to be rock solid is 99 per cent space, and what appears to be empty space is the laboratory of life. We need to tread very carefully if we would attempt to define what is 'real' and what is not.

How, in all this infinity of uncertainty, in this universe that is so very much more than it appears to be, are we to find our way and build our lives on solid ground? What *is* solid?

Inigo, of course, was spared the complications of quantum mechanics and particle physics. But he knew very well that finding solid ground was crucial to the life to which God beckons us. And he knew that there was much more to this challenge than simply keeping the rules and performing the rituals. He knew it was about personal choice, and he discovered for himself that making choices in favour of life is far from easy. So he began his *Exercises* with an invitation to return to first principles, to discover and affirm where the real foundation of our living is to be. Not surprisingly, he called this exercise the 'First Principle and Foundation'. How can it help us today?

A friend shared a joke with me: there were three people, he told me, three people with very different outlooks on life (actually they had different nationalities, but we don't want to offend anyone here!). Let's just say that the first person was something of an entrepreneur, the second was interested in making things, and the third was an introspective dreamer. Well one day these three people came face to face with an elephant. None of them had ever seen an elephant before. The first person, the one with the eye for the quick buck, said to himself: 'I wonder how much money I could make with a creature like that?' The second person, the one who liked making things, said to himself: 'I wonder how I could use a creature like that in my engineering projects?' And the third person, the introspective type, said to himself: 'I wonder what that creature is thinking about *me*?'

Three different reactions, but with one common factor. All three of them were focused on *themselves*. What use is this to *me*? What effect does it have on *me*? What does it think of *me*?

The principle here is quite simply the ego-principle – I am centre stage, and I relate to everything and everyone else only insofar as they affect me. As Louis XIV, the self-styled 'Sun King', famously claimed, 'L'État c'est moi.' I *am* the state, everything has to revolve around me. That is simply how things are.

We wouldn't be so egocentric . . . would we? These are caricatures. And what do caricatures do? They observe a feature of reality, and amplify it. Can we be so sure that our own attitudes do not revolve mainly around ourselves and our own needs and desires? It has been said that the one unique characteristic that distinguishes humankind from the other species is our amazing capacity for self-deception.

Inigo came to the conclusion that the reality of the True Life – its solid underlying principle – is to recognize that our own living revolves around some centre much deeper and greater than ourselves. He would name this centre 'God'. Insofar as we live according to this principle (whereby the Earth revolves around the sun and not the other way round!), we will have a basis for living and choosing that is in harmony with the way things truly are, and not distorted by our own illusions.

When a God-centred approach to life is our underlying principle, then everything that we encounter can be the means of drawing us into closer alignment with the True Life. We are free to receive and welcome all created things in this spirit, without trying to possess them and force them into orbit around ourselves.

So much for the 'principle'. What about the 'foundation'?

The rock and the quicksands

I spent some time in Blundellsands on Merseyside one summer. I especially enjoyed its sandy beach, and used to go there whenever I had a chance. I went there once too often, and found myself sinking into quicksands. Suddenly, out of the blue, I was up to my ankles in shifting sand, and

painfully aware of the powerful suction beneath the soles of
my feet. I managed to extricate myself, but after that little
incident I was extremely careful where I put my feet on that
beach. It was impossible to tell, just from looking at the top
surface of the sand, where it was covering solid rock and
where it was concealing deadly downward forces. Every
step had to be discerned!

Life is like that beach. When we wake up in the morning,
we really don't know what lies ahead. We can't tell, just
from the visible surface of things, where the solid ground is.
But we can learn to *discern*. Morecambe Bay, in the north-
west of England, is notorious for its quicksands and has
been the scene of many tragedies. It is well known and well
publicized there that one cannot cross the wide expanse of
the bay safely without the services of a guide. The guide
knows exactly where the quicksands are and where the
solid ground is located.

What, or who, might act as a guide to us as we cross the
unpredictable sands of life? The 'who?' is easy, at least for
Christians. Jesus describes himself as 'the Way'. To walk
alongside him, in the ways suggested in Chapter 3, is to
have a personal guide. This chapter, however, is more to do
with the 'what?' The 'what', in Ignatian spirituality, is the
tool of discernment, which offers us a set of tools to help us
know ourselves better and discern the best way forward in
every situation. To live true, we need both the personal
guidance of Jesus and the tools of discernment. In the rest
of this chapter we will have a look at what this toolkit
contains.

The discovery of these tools goes back to Inigo's convalescence at Loyola. There, you will recall, he discovered
for himself that some of his daydreams left him feeling flat
and listless, while others seemed to give him new energy.
This observation led him on to notice a series of clues,
which he then used to discern which of the deeper move-

ments stirring in his heart were life-giving, and which were draining him of life. Had he been walking across Morecambe Bay, he might have expressed it as the difference between those inner movements that left him feeling he was standing on solid ground, and those that had the effect of sucking him down into stagnation and self-absorption.

A careful look at these clues will repay our attention.

Clue 1 – the deepest desire

We begin by getting in touch with what we might call our deepest desire. This may come as something of a surprise to readers who have always believed that whatever God's will is about, it is likely to be diametrically opposed to their own. When we speak of the deepest desire, we are referring to what is deep in the core of our being – that part of us where God's dream for us is being shaped. This kind of desiring lies far, far deeper than the list of wants and wishes that we might identify at the more superficial levels of our being. For those whose hearts are, deep down, directed towards God, however they understand God, the deepest desire will be in tune with God's dream for them, and for all creation.

Often the deepest desire of our hearts cannot be expressed in words. It may, however, find eloquent expression in what we choose to do, how we spend our energy. For example, for a keen gardener, one level of desiring may be to maintain a beautiful garden or to grow prize vegetables. At a deeper level, this desire is about being a co-creator, with God, of a beautiful and fruitful earth, which will be a source of joy and sustenance to all. Clearly, such a deep desire would be very much in tune with God's own dream of 'life in all its fullness'.

So how do you get in touch with that deep dream? One

way might be to imagine that you have been told that you have only six months to live. What would you most want to do during this time? What might you want to say to those you will soon be leaving behind? How, specifically, would you want to be remembered? What aspects of your present lifestyle might you want to change? Such a deadline certainly serves to focus the mind and heart. If you allow your imagination to embrace this scenario, it may give you a very clear image of what your heart finds most significant. This is your deepest desire. It points you to the underlying principle that is guiding the way you are living your life.

> Go deep into the cavern of your heart, as suggested above. Can you see the shape of your own deepest desiring?

Clue 2 – God's bias in favour of life

God has desires too! What gives us the confidence to say such things? Well, desire is a form of energy. The power that holds all life in being is a manifestation of a supremely powerful energy. It is foundational to a life of faith that the believer trusts that the energy with which all things are charged is a benevolent power. As Christians, we see in the life of Jesus of Nazareth overwhelming evidence of the benevolence of the energy of God. Jesus, 'God-with-Us', poured his life energy into touching all creation with compassion and healing love. He lived out the bias of God towards all that is life-giving, and he teaches and commissions us to do the same.

On the basis of this evidence, we can say with confidence that it is in the nature of God always to be weaving the most life-giving outcome from whatever we present. Very frequently, what we present is a mess, a tangle of mixed motives, a hornet's nest of problems and compromises. When our children bring us messes like this, we do all we can to draw the more life-giving outcome from it all, perhaps by resolving issues that our children cannot yet handle, or perhaps by lovingly allowing them to work things out for themselves, while we keep a watchful eye out to ensure that they come to no harm. We affirm them every time they choose the wiser, the more loving course; we admonish them, in love, when they make selfish or harmful choices. And so is God with us. Not sending difficulties to 'test' us, but being alongside us in those difficulties, working tirelessly to draw us towards the more life-giving options.

> Look at your own journey through life. Can you see any evidence of where God has 'written straight with crooked lines', drawing life and growth out of what seemed like a tangled mess?

Clue 3 – our own desire to make God's dream come true

Why is it that, in spite of the fact that the world seems so very full of trouble, in practice most of its inhabitants are fundamentally good folk who deeply desire peace, will often go out of their way to help each other, and strive to discover, and live true to, the best in themselves? Surely, it is because a powerful motivation stirs in us to fulfil our potential and help others to fulfil theirs. Whether it is acknowledged or not, and whether or not we would express it in 'religious' language, most people would really love to be part of a dream that is far bigger, and more loving, than anything they can imagine or work out for themselves.

And, although this may not be universally true, it is certainly true of anyone engaged on a spiritual quest – anyone likely to be reading a book like this. Ignatian spirituality fuels our desire to be co-creators of God's reign on earth, and provides us with some invaluable tools for the task.

> Imagine Jesus of Nazareth saying to you personally: 'Come with me. Together we will live God's dream for creation.' Would you want to answer 'Yes', 'No' or 'Maybe later'?

Clue 4 – our moods and feelings

Nevertheless, in spite of our deep desire to build our lives on the rock, we all know the pull of the quicksands, and the first indication you have that you may be walking into quicksands comes to you through the soles of your feet. Believe me. I've tried it! You realize the danger through feeling the downward drag, the suction of the forces lurking deep in this harmless-looking beach. You *feel* it, literally with your sense receptors, transmitted through your central nervous system, to be processed in your brain, and translated into evading action by your muscles.

In the same way our inner moods and feelings can guide us to an awareness of where the quicksands may be in our living, and where we might find solid rock.

When I look back over the days in this kind of way, the word that seems to fit these varying tendencies towards, or away from, the best in myself would be 'movements'. I notice, day after day, that I am subject to inner movements that can bring out the best, or the worst, in me, and all points in between. Naturally, I wish I could always go with the positive movements, and resist the negatives. I very seriously want to find the solid rock in my life, and keep out of the quicksands, but, like St Paul, I frequently end up failing to do the good things I really, deep down, want to do, and perpetrating the very things I most wish I could avoid doing.

Inigo would have called these movements the 'bad spirits' and the 'good spirits', the 'demons' and the 'angels'. Many people today might regard them as simply the movements that go on within our own psyche, prompting us variously towards what is creative (the solid rock) and what is destructive (the quicksands). Whether they are purely subjective, or whether they have an objective and universal reality way beyond our personal realm of consciousness, is a question we don't actually have to answer, but may more wisely allow to remain in the cloud of unknowing. What really matters is not so much what we call these movements, or whether they are objective or subjective, but whether they are basically creative or destructive, and *how we choose to react to them*. Inigo had the wisdom to realize this, and the tools he gives us are as sharp and effective for us today as they were for him in the cave at Manresa five hundred years ago.

So a key tool in the toolkit comes in the shape of our moods and feelings. Its use might be summed up in these questions:

What, today, has felt as though it was sucking you into the quicksands? What was pulling you 'out of orbit', further away from your true self? You might notice this pull, for example, in incidents or reactions that left you feeling a bit at odds with yourself, sensing that you had acted out of something less than the best in yourself. You may sense that somehow these things have depleted the store of love, hope and trust in yourself and in the world.

What, today, has felt as though it was drawing you towards the best in yourself? Such incidents or reactions may have left you feeling a deep sense of the rightness of things. They may have helped to deepen a good relationship, or challenge something that is out of order. They will have added to the store of love, hope and trust in yourself and in the world.

Clue 5 – the roots of the matter

But simply noticing our moods and feelings, and realizing that some of them are indicating a pull away from the true alignment of our hearts, and others indicate a drawing towards it, is only the first step. We now have to discover what is the root cause of our reaction.

If I feel irritated when the woman next door starts her gossiping, or a particular topic of conversation in the family always puts me in a bad mood, what is really going on here? What is the real nature of these quicksands? Perhaps I wish that *I* had more time to spend just chatting. Perhaps a conversation triggers some unresolved fear or anger in me?

If I feel a deep sense of peace about a decision, even though it may have involved painful choices, what does this reveal about the nature of the solid rock in my life? There is a sense of being 'at balance' when we are living true to the best in ourselves. This doesn't give us a pain exemption ticket, but it helps us begin to see the pain in the perspective of a greater good – perhaps new growth, or a deepening of love or compassion.

A 'rubbish day' can be an invaluable map to the terrain of our hearts. Underneath all those minor irritations or major disturbances of our inner sense of peace and wholeness lie the roots of what is impeding us on our journey towards the true life we seek in Christ. These are the warnings on the map that tell us there are quicksands about. They teach us where we need to take avoiding action, consciously working against what tends to pull us down the destructive spiral.

And those moments, often unexpected, that lift us beyond ourselves, perhaps through the kindness of others, or through a glimpse of something so much greater than ourselves and our preoccupations, are the signs on the map that reveal where the solid rock is – the true and trust-worthy foundation, on which we can make our life's choices and decisions.

Inigo speaks frequently of what he calls spiritual *consolation* and *desolation*. These terms come from the Spanish, and ultimately the Latin root, meaning 'with the sun' ('*con*-solation') and 'away from the sun' ('*de*-solation'), and shelves of books have been written about what they mean and how they affect us. In brief, we might say:

- In spiritual consolation, we are, as it were, facing, or focused on, the source of light, the 'otherness' of God. When our focus is on God, we are close to the rock, the solid ground of our being. We can trust our feelings to be guiding us in the true direction of our hearts.
- In spiritual desolation, we are inwardly facing away from the source of light, and focused instead on our own ego-self, our immediate preoccupations. Like the people meeting the elephant, our question is 'How does this affect *me*?' 'How can I make this situation/relation-ship/person fit into *my* system of things?' From this stance, and, as it were, with our back to the source of light, we are in danger of wandering into the quicksands. Our feelings are not a trustworthy guide to our true direction. We are tending to re-make the world in our

own image and for our own convenience, and such a world will not hold!

In his 'First Principle and Foundation', Inigo reminds us that in the core of our being we are created to love, serve and be in right relationship with a centre of gravity at the heart of all creation – whom we might name 'God'.

One useful test of whether we find ourselves in consolation (on the rock) or in desolation (in the quicksands) is this:

> In this particular issue, am I seeking to serve and be in right relationship with God and God's creation, or am I trying to make God and God's creation serve *me*? Where is the centre of gravity around which this issue is revolving for me? Where is my focus?

Clue 6 – the pull of all the lesser attractions

But of course it is never that easy! Would that we could simply live true to the deepest desires of our hearts, and thereby consistently align our lives with God's dream for creation. Unfortunately there is no shortage of lesser attractions along the way – or rather, they are more like *dis*tractions than attractions. They have the power to lure us off course, while we explore their cul-de-sacs, and lose track of the deeper thrust of what means most to us. Ultimately they will fail to satisfy our deeper longings. They are like Inigo's daydreams of the great battles and lovely ladies he would win – initially enticing, but ultimately disappointing. They merely sap our energy and fail to carry us closer to our heart's true goal.

So, our beach is not only infested with quicksands. It is also continually producing *mirages*.

If, in the desert, you are making your way by the right route to the desired destination, and you see what appears to be an oasis, complete with palm trees, away over to the left or right of the true course, what do you do? Many a desert trekker has gone off to the 'oasis', only to find that it melts away as soon as he approaches it. By which time, of course, he has at best wasted a lot of precious time and supplies, in going off course, and at worst he has got completely lost, and is unable to retrace his steps back to the true course.

Mirages, for the spiritual trekker, are those many lesser wants and wishes, cares, preoccupations and distractions that tempt us to go after them and leave what we know is the true course of our hearts' deepest desiring. They are, of course, *illusions*. They will dissolve in our arms, like the oasis on the desert horizon, like Inigo's unsatisfactory daydreams. But we will have invested our energy in pursuing them, and we may have nothing left for the true heart-journey.

The fact that we believe, so strongly, in these illusions (or 'attachments', as they are often called in Ignatian spirituality), doesn't make them either true or real. Some things will never be true, however much we believe in them. Learning to see beyond the illusions, and to resist the pull of the mirages, is the beginning of spiritual freedom, which we will consider in the next chapter.

Putting it into practice

Ignatian spirituality is a very practical guide to the Christian journey. So we might expect that Inigo would include, in his *Exercises*, some hands-on guidance for making choices wisely, and we will not be disappointed. If you are working at a decision in your life right now, you might like to see whether any of these suggestions help you. All are from the *Exercises* directly, or derived from their wisdom.

Weighing up the options

Draw up a two-column list on a sheet of paper. In the left-hand column, make a note of all the advantages of choosing in favour of a particular option. In the right-hand column, note all the disadvantages. Repeat the exercise for all the possible options you are considering. Often a list like this will reveal a clear winner. At the very least it will focus your mind on what is really important to you. If other people are directly affected by the decision, involve them in the process too, perhaps encouraging each person to draw up their own sheets, and then comparing them. This often reveals the real needs and hopes of very different people engaged in the same process.

Testing your choices

Suppose you have discerned that there are two clear options ahead of you (for example, to take a new job or not). Spend a day or two, in your imagination, as if you had definitely decided on the first option. Let yourself imagine in detail how it would feel. As you encounter the everyday patterns of your living, ask yourself 'How will this be in the future, now that I have decided for option X?' Just notice your feelings. They may speak to you with a more profound truth than your mind alone can manage. Now do the same, for a day or two, imagining you have definitely decided in favour of option Y. When you have done an imaginative 'dry run' of each of your options, let your findings help you in the final discernment.

Looking ahead

This is another imaginative exercise. Try to imagine your-self nearing the end of your life. Perhaps you have been told you have only a few months to live. How would you want to make your choice in these circumstances? The proximity of death can focus the mind like nothing else. It can show us what – and who – really matters to us.

Letting the best in you decide

Suppose you could make a spiritual barometer, with a scale indicating how close you are to the true core of your being in any particular issue. At the top of the scale would be 'What the best in me chooses', and at the bottom of the scale would be 'What the worst in me wants'. Take a long, cool, honest look at this barometer, in the light of the choice you are making. On a scale of one to ten, how would you rate your choice? In the light of your 'reading', do you want to modify your decision at all?

The consultant test

Suppose you were asked to advise someone else in your situation – perhaps someone you care for very much, and want the very best for. How would you advise them to respond to the situation you are dealing with?

We are what we choose

If we were asked to summarize in two words the vision into which Jesus of Nazareth beckons us, and the way that leads to that vision, we might use the phrase: 'Choose life'.

Every aspect of Ignatian spirituality is offered as a way to help us keep on making this fundamental choice for life, in our everyday living, in our relationships and in all our journeying. We can only make the choice for life when we are living by a larger principle than mere self-interest. We can only be free to grow into the fullness of life that God dreams for each of us, when we are standing on the solid rock of our being. Only there do we discover the foundation that gives us the freedom to move on, as co-operating companions of the One who is constantly striving to grow our worst into better and our better into best.

In every choice for life (for ourselves and for others), we become a little bit more fully alive. In every choice that is life-denying, for ourselves or for others, we die a little. We are becoming what we choose.

5

Free to Grow

Quicksands certainly focus the mind on that deep under-lying question: 'Where is my real security?' When I get so carried away with the view, or the activities going on around me, or even my own thoughts, I can easily find myself wandering into territory that may prove harmful. Avoiding the quicksands in life involves a high degree of awareness, and the ability to tread lightly, keeping the focus on what really matters and resisting following the surface distractions that present themselves.

Imagine this little scene, which I witnessed one morning on the main road near our home. Two cock pheasants were having a fight, right in the middle of the road. Whatever the scrap was about, they were utterly engrossed in going for each other's jugular. I guess each one was thinking how supremely important it was to get the better of this chal-lenger. What neither of them was thinking was that both of them stood in imminent danger of being flattened by the next car. In the light of the larger situation, the lesser matters might have evaporated.

The scene made me smile . . . until I reflected on how similar my own behaviour can be. I too get totally absorbed in the immediate matter of the moment, and I lose sight of the longer perspective – I go off along the many cul-de-sacs that life presents, and I forget which path I was really trying to follow, and the destination I was actually heading towards. I am no better than the bird-brained pheasants.

The only difference is that they have a good excuse for having bird brains. I have been given rather sharper tools of discernment. You could say the pheasants were up to their necks in the quicksands of mutual conflict.

How might we do a bit better, in our own quicksands?

- Avoiding the quicksands means to tread lightly.
- When you tread lightly on an uncertain beach, you detect the presence of the shifting sand.
- When you can detect it, you can avoid it.
- To be able to avoid it, you have to be free of any undue hankering to walk precisely there – maybe because 'there' is a place that holds some powerful attraction for you.

This level of freedom doesn't come cheap. Our desires for all those lesser things that have the potential to lead us into quicksands are not going to go away easily. We are going to have to work at it. To do so, we need to develop three skills in particular. Ignatian spirituality has a lot of wisdom to offer on the nature of these skills.

- Staying focused on what is really coming from the core of our being. Inigo can help with this, in an exercise he calls 'The Two Standards', which we will explore a bit more fully later in this chapter.
- Distinguishing between what is life-giving (the solid rock) and what is life-denying or life-threatening (the quicksands). This is the art of *discernment*.
- Sitting lightly to all that happens, with a readiness to let go of what is not, or is no longer, leading us closer to our true selves in God. This is the art of *detachment*.

These three skills, faithfully practised until they become an integral part of who we are and how we live and make our choices, are the basis of a freedom that is also perhaps best illustrated by means of a story:

One day, in a far off land, there was a terrible war. The innocent people of that land were reduced to starvation, and in their fear they fled in droves, pursued by a cruel enemy army. It happened that a holy hermit lived in that same land. He realized that the enemy was advancing, burning down the people's homes and taking their lives. He saw his people fleeing. The hermit stayed in his cave, refusing to let fear drive him out.

Soon the enemy soldiers reached the cave. When they found him there, pursuing his life of prayer, unperturbed, they demanded to know who he was. When told his name, the commander of the soldiers raised his sword to the hermit's throat, saying: 'Don't you realize that I am a man with the power to extinguish your life, without batting an eyelid?' To which the hermit replied: 'Don't you realize that I am a man who can let you do that, without batting an eyelid?' The soldiers moved on, leaving the hermit to his life with God.

The hermit demonstrates the three skills: he stays focused on what really matters most to him at the core of his being, and does not allow fear to drive him off course. From that still point at the centre of his being he is able to distinguish clearly between what is life-giving and what is destructive. He is able to find the strength, at that still point, to resist what is life-denying. And he is able to sit lightly to lesser desires, even the desire for a longer life, if that is the cost of retaining this deep inner freedom.

We might explore this way of looking at things by making, in prayerful imagination, a journey of our own. It is a familiar one, which we know from scripture, but we might fruitfully make some connections with life in our modern, wounded, wonderful world. On this imaginative journey, as in our own personal journeying, we meet with both the powerfully transformative, and the desperately destructive elements of human experience. To be aware of these two conflicting movements within us and around us is to begin to discern which movement we really wish to follow, and to make our choices, both large and small, in the light of that wisdom. It is the beginning of the inner freedom which, alone, will give us space to grow into the fullness of our being, in God.

To help us do this, let's take a walk on Mount Tabor with Jesus and three of his closest friends. Jesus is climbing the mountain, in order to pray. When they reach the summit Jesus undergoes a mysterious transformation. He appears to them to be radiant with an inner light that makes his whole being shine with a brilliance that dazzles them, and they see Moses and Elijah, one each side of their Lord. A cloud descends, veiling the very presence of God, and out of the cloud they hear the voice of the Father: 'This is my chosen one: listen to him.' They are so overawed that they want to capture the moment and hold it in their grasp forever. In our day and age, they would no doubt have tried to photograph the scene. As it is, they suggest pitching three tents, one each for Jesus, Elijah and Moses; but before the momentary glory can be seized, it is gone from sight.

If we allow ourselves to inhabit this scene, and at the same time reflect on a very different, but strangely similar incident in recent history, we might glimpse something of the nature of both our best and our worst tendencies and the very different effects they have upon us. These parallel narratives give us some insight into what Inigo called 'the two standards' – the contrast between following what leads to life and being seduced into what is ultimately destructive of life.

Two lights, two clouds, two tents

It was 6 August, the Feast of the Transfiguration in the liturgical calendar. In the world's calendar it was the anniversary of the dropping of the atomic bomb on the Japanese city of Hiroshima. I couldn't help making the connection as I reflected on these two narratives, so strangely linked by the chance of a date.

Both these stories, the one from the Christian Gospel, the other from the Second World War, are completely over the top in the way they stretch credibility to its limits. Who would believe his friends when they reported that Jesus had been transformed into a dazzling presence of light on a mountain-top, appearing to them with Moses and Elijah alongside him? Wouldn't people say the heat had affected their minds and made them susceptible to hallucinations? And who would believe that wholesale, lingering, malignant, generation-leaping death would drop from the skies upon hundreds of thousands of innocent men, women and children – some of them yet unborn? Had the heat of war not surely addled our brains and caused us to take leave of our senses and forget the first principles of what it means to be human?

Yet there they are: two stories that can help us to be more aware of both our life-giving and our life-denying tendencies, and help us discern the difference. Perhaps these stories serve us well in this regard precisely because they *are* so over the top. We don't, after all, see visions like the transfiguration, do we . . . ? Nor are we responsible for atrocities such as the bombing of Hiroshima, are we . . . ? So why is it that people who may well go out of their way to declare that they 'are not religious' *do* in fact experience mountain-top moments in their lives that continue to affect the way they live, long after the moment has passed? And why is it that perfectly decent men and women *can* in practice behave in sub-human ways when they are put into uniform and ordered to kill their fellow creatures?

The answer, certainly as Inigo would see it, lies in the perpetual conflict between the creative and the destructive movements within our hearts – the good and evil spirits, as he calls them. We could also describe them as the 'best' and the 'worst' within us.

Perhaps I might share with you the reflections that arose for me on that day, 6 August, because they may be helpful in leading us further into this matter of discernment.

First the two lights:

The one is a blinding, sickening flash, death-dealing, and the fruit of fear and hatred. It is hypnotic in its power, drawing all eyes to gaze, quite literally, upon their own destruction, to become fixed to the terror and the brilliance and charged with the destructive energy that will contaminate their whole being.

The other light momentarily transfigures a man who lives completely true to the best in himself. He appears to his friends to be literally transformed by the light of that inner truth. This light illuminates the whole course of a people's sacred history (we learn that Moses and Elijah are included in its halo). It displaces everything except its own perfect radiance and causes those who fall within its power to shade their eyes in reverence.

It is the difference between radiance and radiation!

Do you have any memories of your own, of moments when your life's landscape was momentarily transfigured by the sweeping beam of God's love, or the breathtaking beauty of creation, or the deep warmth of human communion? Just remember these sacred times of transfiguration and let their light penetrate the height and depth and breadth of your being. This kind of light is shed by your 'angels' – the life-giving moments in your heart. It reveals the traces of your deepest and finest dreams, the dreams that God shares with you. Let it illumine the path for you – the path that shows you the more loving, the more true, the more Christ-like thing to do next.

Now, in the confidence that the transfiguration light has more power within you than any lesser glow, recall any aspects of your life that feel more like the death-flash over Hiroshima (though probably less dramatic). Recall anything that has transfixed you with fear or with a compulsive desire that your deeper heart knew was destructive. Don't be afraid to acknowledge, if necessary, that there have been more destructive flashes than transforming lights – you would not be alone in this truth. These lights reflect the power of the destructive movements within you, with their capacity to hold you captive in ways that seduce you into choices that are not leading to life.

Finally, in the honesty of your own heart, and in the presence of your God, reflect on which of these lights you choose to nurture, and which you would want to work against, and then ask God for the grace to follow these desires in practical ways.

And the two clouds:

Both the clouds are charged with enormous power. The one rises like a mushroom, spreading its deadly spores across the world. The mushroom cloud of a nuclear explosion has become a household image. Everyone knows what it means and what it portends. Everyone shrinks in fear of its shadow.

The other cloud descends gently, like a blanket, enveloping everything we thought we knew and everything we think we are, wrapping us in deep mystery, as if to incubate a new beginning. Its power is the power of life, but how many people know the coming of the cloud of God's presence? Perhaps only those who learn to surrender their lesser selves, their ego-selves, those who learn to tread lightly on the earth, holding on to nothing, but with hands and hearts open to receive everything? It is a scary place to find oneself – the cloud of unknowing, the dark mystery of God, in which our own knowledge leads us nowhere; but it is also the creative space where new life is brought forth.

It is the difference between the shadow of menace and the shade that gives us space to become who we truly are.

What do these two cloud-images mean for *you*?

What aspects of your life hang over you like a threatening presence – perhaps menacing relationships or situations beyond your immediate control, or possibly stirrings within your own heart that disturb and unsettle you and that you would wish to turn away from if you could? These clouds are the dwelling place of your 'demons' – the destructive movements within and around you.

Which parts of your life feel more like an enveloping, sheltering blanket, which protects the tender core of your being as it grows more and more towards the person God dreamed into being when God created you? This kind of creative cloud may leave you deeply mystified, and unsure of the way ahead, but it will also give you the space to surrender the 'less' of your own flawed vision into the 'more' of God's vision for you. It is the cloud where your 'angels' dwell, the secret source of your creative energy.

In the stillness of your heart, acknowledge the presence of both these clouds, as you ask for the grace to work against the darkness that destroys, and surrender yourself to the creative power of God's overshadowing love.

And finally, two kinds of tent:

It happened that on the night of 6 August that year, I had a sleepless night. There was a full moon, and I was staying in the apartment of a relative, in the middle of a busy capital city. The windows were uncurtained, to allow more ventilation on this hot, sticky summer night. I lay awake, watching the moon make her way right across the city, traversing the night from one extreme of my vision to the other, tracing an invisible arc across the flat horizon of the city lights.

The moon's journey through the night reminded me of my own inner journey, and the tents that I pitch at every opportunity, as the disciples wanted to do on Mount Tabor, in the hope of preserving the magic moment. I realized that whenever I feel the pull of some, usually inconsequential, little magnet that happens to attract me, I 'pitch a tent' to catch it and keep it contained, and in my control. What is in the tent may be something quite trivial, for example a book I hoard possessively and refuse to lend, for fear that it might never return! Or it might be a big issue in my life, such as a home, or a career, or a significant relationship, which I hedge around with so many 'belt and braces' securities for fear of losing it: for example, I may cripple myself financially with insurance policies, or damage my physical or emotional health through overwork, to secure my career prospects, or compromise my own integrity for the sake of hanging on to a dependent relationship. Tents like this stop me moving on. They become chains around my ankles. They are the place where my 'demons' find refuge, where I make space for my destructive negative tendencies and give them safe lodging.

And there are other unhelpful tents that I pitch along my way. Tents that I flee to when I am hurting, to nurse my pain, and to escape the need to face its causes. Tents like these only pull me deeper and deeper into myself and make it harder and harder to move on to new growth.

Tents don't have to be like this. They don't have to be butterfly nets to catch and hold the fleeting moment, as the friends of Jesus try to do on Mount Tabor. They don't have to be escape routes from life's difficulties. Above all, they don't have to be *fixed*.

A very different kind of tent would be one that I carry on my back, as a *temporary* shelter along life's journey. Prayer can be a tent of this kind, and so can a conversation with a trusted soul-friend. Any space, any occasion, any encounter that draws us closer to the heart of ourselves and of each other is a meeting place with God, no less than the Ark of the Covenant, the Tent of Meeting, that the children of Israel carried with them through the desert – a portable God, who accompanies all life in its confused wandering, manifesting the holy amid the ordinary, charging every particle of creation with sacredness.

Are you aware of any 'fixed containers' in your life that you would find it hard to relinquish, or any 'butterfly nets' in which you have tried in vain to capture life's magic moments? Do you feel you have become permanently lodged in a place, or a mindset, that was only meant to be a temporary shelter along the way?

By contrast, what does the holy tent of meeting mean for you? Where and what are your sacred spaces? How do these 'tents' energize your journey and facilitate your moving on? Take time to reflect on their shape and form for you. In them your 'angels' dwell.

A transfiguration on Irish soil

I happened by chance to be in Ireland in June 2003 while the Special Olympics were in progress. This celebration of human vitality was one of the most moving events I can remember. The Games were for people with special needs. For some, simply to pick up a bean bag, or to roll over on a mat, were mammoth tasks, demanding all the energy and determination they could muster. As I reflect back on that happy coincidence, I am reminded of the light, the cloud and the tents of transfiguration in a vivid contemporary way, and I see there too a helpful guide to discerning between my angels and my demons.

The two-week event began with a display of *light*. The opening ceremony was a brilliant festival of life. Nelson Mandela presided, and the Irish people, with one heart and one voice, welcomed the participants. The significance of this was not lost on anyone. Mandela, and his people, know the depths of human loss and suffering, and so do the Irish people. Their welcome to these special needs guests was heartfelt in the truest sense. The lights that burst forth over the arena were transfiguration lights – shining forth a radiance that the darkness had not overcome. And I remembered the destructive lights of gunfire, searchlights and border flares that so many of those present had also known in their lives, but so overwhelmingly outshone here by the light of life. The 'angels' were certainly present in power that evening, and the 'demons' were relegated to the sidelines. What a reason to rejoice!

And many of those present also knew what it means to live under a *cloud* – the mushroom clouds of apartheid, of sectarian violence, of social and political injustice and of the marginalization of the physically or mentally disadvantaged. Yes, there were enough clouds there to cover a world, let alone a sports arena. The 'demons' could have had a field-day, but another cloud was present in even greater power. It was the kind of warm and welcoming cloud that enfolds people like a mother hen. It was even a vocal cloud – as became obvious when the crowds thundered forth their applause for the competitors. It reached its peak when the Iraqi team entered the arena. The Irish people, themselves so war-torn and battle-wearied, rose to their feet and gave these new victims of conflict and oppression a standing ovation. It wasn't too difficult to hear, with the ears of the heart, the words of God coming from this cloud – 'These are my beloved ones. Listen to them.'

And the *tents*? The history of so many of those present was one of the refugee: fleeing from hostility, aggression, discrimination; hiding from the scathing comment and the patronizing stare; living from hand to mouth. But here in Ireland they discovered other tents. Many of the towns and cities of Ireland – north and south – were officially hosting competing nations' teams. In my travels that week I came upon the evidence – 'Navan welcomes Belgium', 'Newry welcomes Iceland', and so many more. The welcome wasn't confined to official banners. It was rooted and grounded in the homes of the people of those towns. This is what one such family told me: 'We were a bit nervous. We didn't know whether they would speak the language, or like the food, or feel at home, but we did our best. And do you know, they *loved* it. They ate every crumb – they relished the puddings! And they would break out in song and dance

– just like that.' 'You see,' my informant continued, 'they have so little going for them, that they seem to tread *lightly* on the earth, and when you do that, you really begin to live the present moment. You really begin to *live!*'

I believe all those guests will always remember the trail of welcome tents that the Irish pitched for them. Angel tents. And I am told that is why angels can fly – because they take themselves so lightly!

The dressing-up game

But don't imagine that the demons are going to take defeat lightly! Remember, we are dealing here with energies we don't understand – we only notice their effects on us. What is destructive can very easily appear in the guise of something wholly life-giving. For example, a genuine concern for the safety and well-being of our families can be a cloak under which excessive fear can lurk. Fear can lead to deep-rooted distrust, which in turn can lead to violent 'pre-emptive strikes' against those around us. The demons have got in through the back door, and they are incredibly hard to evict. Similarly, the desire for peace and harmony, undoubtedly good in itself, can lead to compromise of personal integrity, and even to downright deception. What is essentially good and life-giving can be hijacked by destructive forces. 'The price of freedom is eternal vigilance.'

An everyday tool for practising discernment

In Chapter 2 we looked at the daily prayer of reflection, sometimes called 'The Examen', or 'The Review of the Day'. This form of meditation can very helpfully be expanded to include a review of any evidence during the day of the 'angels' or 'demons':

What parts of the day have made you feel more alive?
Have you noticed any shafts of 'transfiguration light' in
the day? Have you felt the warmth of God's presence
enfolding you in any way, like the cloud of wonder in
the Gospel story, most probably through the words or
actions of another human person? Has anything
happened that has helped you to move on in your
journeying? Have you been a source of light, or warmth,
or guidance to anyone else?

*What parts of the day have left you feeling drained of
energy?* Have you found your gaze becoming fixed on
what is life-denying or even harmful, to yourself or
others? Have you noticed any mushroom clouds menacing your deeper peace, or that of others? Is there
any way you can work against their effects by making
choices that lead back to life? Have you found yourself
trying to hang on to something, or someone, you were
afraid to lose?

Don't judge yourself. Simply notice and acknowledge
what you find of these inner movements during your
day. Ask for the grace to nourish what is leading to life,
and work against what is destructive.

Travelling light

I travelled to Canada one year. I was visiting two widely
separated regions, one coastal and temperate and the
other mountainous and exposed. And I was going to be
spending some time in fairly formal company, and some
time wandering freely in the Rockies. I would need – so I
thought – a wide variety of different gear. Result: two large

suitcases that I could barely lift; a battle with the check-in scales at every airport en route, and, at the end of the trip, the realization that I had actually needed less than half of the stuff I carted with me. Lesson: you won't move very far or very fast if you can't lift up your own baggage!

Since then I try really hard to travel light. Sometimes it is simple, and I know now that small is beautiful when it comes to suitcases and backpacks. I am finding it relatively easy to live without some of the things I used to think were indispensable. But when it comes to the inner journey of my heart, I am still paying for excess baggage all the way.

There are all kinds of inner baggage that accumulate. The hardest to deal with is the weight of personal attachments. For example: I 'can't' participate in something I would really like to do, because I am afraid of failure, or I am reluctant to get too involved. When I was a child my mother used to tell me: 'There's no such word as "can't"'. 'The only thing you can't do', she said, 'is get the toothpaste back into the tube once you've squeezed it out.' Perhaps she meant more by that comment than she guessed. The word 'can't' usually translates more accurately into 'won't' or 'daren't'. And the only thing we genuinely *can't* do is go backwards. Every possibility for moving forwards is open to us.

Even so, the drag of those many 'attachments', in the form of excessive fears, or an overriding desire for a comfortable life, or any other attitudes that hold us captive, are powerful. They are like the heavy bags that stop us in our tracks at the airport check-in. I once witnessed a contretemps between a would-be traveller and an airline official. 'Sorry, sir,' the official said, 'but that cabin bag is too big and too heavy to go on board. It's a safety hazard.' The protests came pouring out. 'But it's no bigger than other people's . . . Your scales must be faulty . . . Other airlines don't make all this fuss . . . I'll hold it on my lap . . . I *need* it!' But the official stood his ground: 'With that baggage, sir, you are simply not going on board this aircraft. You either travel without it, or you stay here with it. Your choice.' End of story.

Inigo would have appreciated this kind of check-in battle. He would have recognized the kind of inner baggage that stops us journeying on in the quest to live true. And he would have recognized the arguments that our many false selves send up against our true selves; all those excuses for choosing from a place which is not – and we know it! – the best in us. He even has a very wise suggestion for dealing with this kind of attachment. We will never, he recognizes, free ourselves of wanting these many lesser gratifications and satisfactions by beating ourselves up or going on a guilt trip about it. The only thing that will free us is to nurture an *even deeper* and *more passionate* desire for something more powerfully true. We will only discover that the many mirages are illusions if we keep our hearts fixed on the greater visions – the deepest desires – that are energizing our lives.

A couple of examples: Jenny was terrified of flying. This fear was becoming obsessive, and it stopped her from ever taking a holiday abroad. Then her only son went to live overseas. Energized by her deep desire to visit her son, she was able to overcome her fear of flying. Jim was an alcoholic. For years his family had tried to cope with the consequences of his addiction, baling him out of every destructive situation his drinking caused. Eventually their own strength broke down, and they couldn't take any more. The family was on the brink of breaking up. At this point Jim realized just how much he stood to lose. Though it was a hard, uphill struggle, he was able to focus all his energy on the deep desire to retain the love and respect of his family, and, with help, move beyond the addiction.

Neither of these (fictitious) examples is suggesting that

such situations are easily resolved, or that any blame is to be attached to the person in the grip of the fear or the addiction. I offer them only as illustrations of the wisdom that we will not be liberated by the 'stick' of punishment or guilt, but by the 'carrot' of the greater vision – a wisdom that Inigo invites us to explore and to make our own, in and through the challenge of the *Exercises*, which themselves reflect the challenge of the gospel.

How is your baggage looking? Is there anything around in your own experience that weighs so heavily on your heart that it is preventing you from moving on? Can you name this baggage to yourself, and perhaps to a trusted friend? To be able to say, in complete honesty, 'This is who I am, and this is my problem' is a proven first step on the long road towards inner freedom.

Choosing what leads to life

This chapter can at best be regarded as a mere taster of the deep and often unconscious movements at work within us, that can draw us closer and closer to the best we are born to, but can also drag us further away from that 'best', down into destructive spirals that suck us, like quicksands, into the worst we are capable of. These are principles that underlie the search for authentic spiritual freedom. Ignatian spirituality offers powerful tools to assist us in this quest.

Such principles in effect give us permission to seek out and nourish all that leads to life, and to leave aside, or resist all that drags us in the opposite direction. You might think that this would be unarguably good news for anyone who is seeking to live by the Christic vision articulated by and embodied in Jesus of Nazareth. Yet to try to live by these principles may lead us into big questions. What, for example, if aspects of church life and 'religion' themselves are not, or are no longer, leading us to life, but even possibly impeding our journey with God? To suggest such a possibility is to invite censure, yet this is unquestionably the experience of many faithful Christians.

Ironically, this saint of the Church (albeit a saint who, like many others, was demonized before he was canonized) has, as it were, given permission to sit lightly to, or even to reject, those aspects of life – including aspects of church life and teaching (though he wouldn't have admitted this in his own day and age) – if they are not leading us closer to the heart of God as revealed in Jesus of Nazareth.

Not everything we are taught has its origins in the bedrock of our being – in God. Much of it is imposed by man-made institutions, whether social, political or ecclesiastical, with very human, and sometimes very questionable motives. As I sift through some of the received 'truths' of our society, or the doctrines, rules and regulations that have been built into the edifice of the organized religions, the line from *Porgy and Bess* wafts through my mind: 'It ain't necessarily so!'

If you find yourself in this place of questioning, wondering increasingly just how much of what is being received has its origins in God and how much is coming from very flawed and human agents, then you may want to spend quality time sifting through your own experience, asking for the grace to discern what to keep, what to set aside and what to resist. No one can do this for you, though such a discernment process is best carried out with an understanding, non-judgemental, and *non-directive* listening companion alongside you.

I would merely leave you with one little litmus test: 'Does this (doctrine, rule, practice, etc.) stem from fear or from love? Is it leading to an increase of love, trust and hope for myself and for the *entire* community of the human family and all creation, or is it leading to division, distrust and despair?'

The Taizé chant reminds us, beautifully, 'Ubi caritas, ibi Deus est' ('Where there is love, there is God') The converse is also true: anything that is feeding on our fears and guilt, setting us apart from one another, operating exclusion zones or imposing threats and sanctions, not just for this life, but for whatever might follow after, is not inspired by the Holy Spirit. Jesus challenged the institutions of his time when they were leading people away from the simple love of God. His twenty-first-century companions may have to do so too, but we do well to do so with great care, deep love, and ongoing prayerful discernment.

In Chapter 6 we will take a look at how this challenging spirituality is being lived out in practice, turning the contemplation of God's love into Christ-like action on behalf of the needs of God's world.

6

Prayer that Works

'Please do not kill my broken heart . . .' Thus pleads an Ethiopian refugee, Yilma Tafere. It is the cry of one refugee, but it could be the cry of an entire planet. It demands a response. Contemplating the heartbreak is not enough, even when that contemplation happens before a lighted candle in a holy place. The contemplation has to give rise to action.

This particular cry penetrated the heart of Pedro Arrupe, then (in 1980) the Father General of the Society of Jesus. Contemplating the devastation being experienced at the time in Africa and Asia, he responded by canvassing the Jesuit regional superiors on what might be *done* to bring some relief to this kind of suffering. It transpired that many Jesuits were already working with refugees in their local areas. Arrupe's immediate response was to establish the Jesuit Refugee Service (JRS) to co-ordinate and facilitate this work world-wide.

A two-pronged approach was adopted. The two prongs could be labelled 'faith' and 'justice'. 'Faith' didn't mean creeds and doctrines. It meant being faithfully alongside those who were suffering. It meant solidarity. It meant carrying the hope for those whom life had rendered 'hopeless'. 'Justice' didn't mean 'judgement', either human or divine. It meant actively seeking real and practical solutions to the injustices that brought about the suffering in the first place. This approach later became known as the 'head and feet approach', and it characterizes the entire Jesuit social apostolate. It is all about living with those who are margin-alized, while at the same time working at the highest levels to secure a more just arrangement of the world's resources and power. And the stem from which both these branches grow is the love of God – the deep desire to live true to the True Life embodied in Jesus of Nazareth, 'so that others might live'.

Of course, most of us are not Jesuits, and certainly the Jesuits would claim no monopoly on faith and justice. This is a call to every member of the human family. How do we translate it into a response that brings life? In this chapter we will look at some of the practical ways that an Ignatian perspective can help us do this.

We might begin by taking a good look at what the words of the chapter heading mean to us. 'Prayer that works' is a phrase that is loaded down with baggage. However far we think we have moved on from our childhood images and expectations of God, there is still, in most of us, a strong unconscious undercurrent that expects 'God' to 'answer' our prayers. Effective prayer would, in this world-view, be identical with prayer that is *answered*, preferably in the way that we think best. I remember vividly a time when a relative of mine was searching for new directions in her spiritual journey. I had it all worked out – how God should manage this situation. I even had it sorted which faith com-munity she might join, and requested God to send along the right kind of contact person for her. All God needed to do was sign along the dotted line and deliver the goods. God didn't do it my way at all! God's arrangements, when they began to become apparent, diverged widely from what I had so carefully thought out, and, as it turned out, proved to be costly to me in ways I could never have imagined.

I am shocked to realize that just a few years ago, I was still operating, unconsciously, with an image of God that was so much a projection of my own requirements. With hindsight, I might describe my 'god' at the time as some-thing of an operations manager – the one with the power to implement my wishes if and when I couldn't manage it myself. There are countless variations on this theme. We can find ourselves praying to a god whom we envisage as the providing parent, or the rescuer, or even the magician. Or we can live in dread of a god who is the censuring head-teacher, the ever-watchful policeman, the vengeful judge and jury. The problem seems to be that once we get fixed on such an image of God, our prayer becomes just another expression of that false image. So we pray for a wish list of favours to be granted, or for deliverance from some intractable situation, or we try to appease a god of retribu-tion by carrying out religious observances or by making sacrificial offerings of our time and money. Not that there is anything wrong with these things in themselves. The problem lies with our underlying view of who God is, and how we are in relation to God.

No image of God will ever be complete, of course, because God is infinite mystery, beyond name, image or description. Nevertheless, we are human creatures, and images necessarily define the way we see things. The image that is at the heart of Ignatian spirituality is of a God who calls us into active partnership in the evolving of a radically new way of being fully human, in the ways we have already explored in earlier chapters. It is a vision that sees us as co-workers, those who labour with God, enabling God's dream to become incarnate in our personal circumstances, our own time and place. How might we put this into prac-tice? In this chapter we will look at some of the possibilities, pioneered and modelled by the Jesuits and grounded very much in the real life of a real world. The 'head and feet' approach can give us some clues, except that we should perhaps extend it to: 'Heart, head and feet'. It challenges us to exercise our discipleship in three specific ways:

- By *listening* (to God, to each other, to the needs of the world and to our own hearts)
- By faithfully *accompanying* (those who are searching, those who are hurting)
- By *embodying* the values and attitudes of Jesus of Nazareth in our own circumstances and our own place and time

Listening – the ecumenical elephant

I am the proud guardian of a Sri Lankan elephant. He comes in ten parts, each part a different shape and colour, and he is a wooden jigsaw puzzle. Apart from being a very satisfying toy, he also doubles as an exercise in ecumenism. His various parts can be distributed among people of differing views and practices, whether religious, social or political, who can then be invited to put the elephant together again, each contributing his or her own unique part to the exercise.

The message is obvious: none of us alone possesses the answer to anything. If we are going to grow in an understanding and practice of what it means to be fully human, we are going to have to put our individual contributions together. This will mean letting go of the illusion that our part is the whole. It will mean that the unique shape and size of who we think we are will be superseded by much bigger shapes, sizes and ways of looking at things – a process of integration that will nevertheless honour and retain the uniqueness of every part. It will mean facing crucial choices about what matters more to us: to hold on to the part we think we possess, or to grow into the discovery of what a greater wholeness might be about.

And when we have put our different parts together, and the elephant is complete, needing every part, but no longer resembling any of them in its final form, we will recognize that we still don't have 'the elephant', but only a representation of an elephant, in painted wood. And so it is, surely, in our attempts to capture the reality of 'God'. Each of us will have a different 'take' on God, and to get anywhere near a full picture, we will need to bring all our partial understandings and experiences together. Even then, we won't have 'got' God, but we will have learned a great deal about the value of the other parts of the jigsaw, and we will have gained the humility to know that we do not, and cannot, *know* the mystery of God, let alone define and prescribe how that mystery works.

What do these jigsaw pieces mean in practice? Perhaps they can guide us, playfully, into the art of listening. One of the human experiences that was greatly valued and encouraged by Inigo was the art of 'spiritual conversation'. This may sound daunting, and the very last thing you need on a Friday evening at the bar. In fact, it turns out to be something a bit like 'writing prose', that you've probably been doing for years, but never knew it.

Can you recall any times when someone has had the grace and the patience to listen to you, with an open heart, and without any judgement or any compulsion to ply you with advice, as you shared something of deep concern or importance to you? How did you feel? In hindsight, how would you value such experience?

Have you yourself ever been the listener in such an encounter? What were the circumstances at the time? What do you think encouraged the other person to open his or her heart to you? In what ways would you say this encounter was enriching to yourself? In what ways may it have enriched the other person?

We tend to assume, perhaps, that 'spiritual conversations' are very earnest undertakings, and even way out of our league. Quite the opposite is true. If you think back for a moment over your life experience, you may well discover that there have been countless significant conversations, many of which will have taken place in apparently unlikely places – in the office, at the social or sports club, at the gym, in the kitchen, on the bus, in the pub – the possibilities are endless. Important conversations, during which the participants are exploring issues that matter to them very deeply, tend to have certain defining characteristics:

- They happen when the participants are feeling at ease, and relaxed. This means that they often arise spontaneously, rather than because 'an appointment has been arranged'. If we find ourselves in the role of listener, then we may well be caught off guard – not really ready at all to deal with the issues involved. This is almost certainly a gift, not a drawback. When we think we can deal with other people's problems, we are probably not going to listen very well – we will be too busy working out our answers. The focus will be on ourselves, rather than on the person we are with.
- They happen within a relationship of *equality*. Ideally (in terms of transactional analysis), the underlying relationship should be one of 'I'm OK, you're OK', and not 'I'm OK, but you've got a problem, so let me help you'. Spiritual conversations are not confessionals or counselling sessions. To go back to the elephant, they are the means whereby one part of the jigsaw can become open to another, in the full recognition that each part is uniquely important in itself and for the whole.
- They can develop into a special kind of friendship. The Celts called this spiritual friendship 'soul friendship', and they valued it above every other form of human inti-

macy. A soul friend is someone with whom you can share what is deepest in your heart, and know that all you share will be held in trust and confidence, and received without judgement or any attempt to 'direct' you.

But to be able to listen, with full and loving attention, to another, we need also to learn to listen to our own hearts, and to develop a sensitive awareness of the movements within ourselves – both those that are leading us towards the best in us, and those that are potentially pulling us away from our best. We need to learn to listen to the nudgings of God within us. The more sensitively we can do this, the more lovingly we will be able to offer a listening heart to others.

And there is another dimension to the art of listening. It could be called 'listening to the signs of the times'. When we are at work, or with family or friends, we are constantly tuned in, not just to what is being said, but, even more importantly, to what *isn't* being said. We all learn to read body language, and to fine-tune our own reactions and behaviour to all that is going on around us. Reading the 'signs of the times' is about extending this art to the larger world around us. It is about getting in touch with the invisible currents under the immediate surface of our society, and discerning, at this level, what is leading us towards a fuller humanity, and what is diminishing our human-ness. In each of us there is a potential mystic and a potential prophet. The mystic intuits what is really going on beneath the surface of things, notices the divine amid the ordinary, and sees others with God's eyes. The prophet addresses what the mystic sees, challenging all that is threatening to undermine humanity's journey towards life-in-all-its-fullness, and encouraging all that is nourishing and empowering that journey.

Take a few minutes to reflect on your own 'inner mystic' and 'inner prophet'. What is your mystic seeing? How does your prophet feel moved to respond? Which tides and currents seem to be influencing the world around you – your personal circle, the world you work in, the world of nations, and the arena of all creation? Which currents are helpful, and which are harmful, to the family of creation? Is there any way to turn your reactions into actions? You might like to share your findings with a friend or group of friends.

Accompanying – power cut strikes stateside

When I reflect on the ministry of *accompanying*, I am reminded of a (true) story I once heard about a rather disastrous power cut that pitched the city of New York into blackness one night. Everything failed. There was no street lighting, no traffic lights, no nothing. The city was reduced to blind panic, as people groped their way around in the darkness, trying to avoid the traffic (no mean feat at the best of times in New York) and find their way home in a cityscape that had been robbed of all its familiar landmarks.

Pandemonium reigned, but in all of the confusion, one man went on his way, undeterred. People noticed that he remained calm amid the confusion, and made his way steadily across busy roads, and seemed to be finding his way home unerringly. Some of them spoke to him as he waited at a kerbside for a safe moment to cross the highway.

'Surely you're not going to try and cross without the lights?' they exclaimed. 'You'll be killed, for sure.'

'What's the problem?' the man responded. 'This is my normal route home. I know it like the back of my hand.'

'But all the lights are out,' they cried.

'Well, I wouldn't know about that,' he said quietly. 'I'm blind.'

And so it happened that a blind man took them safely across the road, relying on the ears he knew he could trust, and his intuitive knowledge of the right direction.

Spiritual companionship is a bit like that. The person doing the accompanying doesn't attempt to direct or instruct, let alone to 'fix' things, but simply walks alongside. You know when you have found a good spiritual companion, because you can sense that they are walking their own pathway with God with intuitive wisdom, trusting the map inside their own heart – a map that will have been discerned through years of prayer and reflection. The companion certainly doesn't have to have 'got it all together'. Far from it: a wounded healer is the best healer; a blind guide is the best guide. A good companion knows, all too well, that she hasn't 'arrived'. The thing about a blind guide is that he doesn't depend on artificial light. His security, in the dark times, rests on something that remains solid when human props break down.

Spiritual companionship is a ministry very close to Inigo's heart, and one which has been greatly fostered and furthered by modern Jesuits. It takes 'listening' a stage further, and reflects the ancient Celtic ministry of 'soul friendship' (the *anam cara*). A soul friend is one who walks alongside, accompanying the spiritual journey, listening with loving attention, without judgement. The ancient Celts held the ministry of soul friendship to be a self-evident necessity on the spiritual journey. 'A person without a soul friend,' they declared, 'is like a body without a head.'

In today's world the practice of this gentle companionship is growing. Increasing numbers of people are being trained (often by the Jesuits) to accompany others along their spiritual path. The essence of such training is to encourage active listening skills and to impress upon would-be companions the importance of not getting in the way in the relationship between God and the pilgrim. They are taught to listen closely and sensitively to anything the pilgrim freely chooses to share, and to reflect back to the pilgrim any aspects of the conversation that seem to be especially loaded or significant. The pilgrim then has the opportunity to explore those issues more deeply if he so wishes. Soul friendship is a gift that one Christian pilgrim can offer to another. In its essence it is a simple, person-to-person encounter, sustained, usually, over some period of time, as the relationship deepens, and the pilgrim's trust grows.

It does, however, have its 'professional' aspect. All spiritual companions should consider themselves absolutely bound by the rule of total confidentiality, and should also be aware of the ethical guidelines governing the way spiritual companionship is conducted. This doesn't mean that training is necessarily either extensive or expensive. Prayer companions with a few weeks' training, provided they have the necessary aptitude and integrity and the gift of empathy, are well able to accompany others as long-term soul friends or in shorter retreats offered in daily-life situations. In its more professional reaches, soul friendship is often called 'spiritual direction', which is an unfortunate misnomer, since whatever it is about, it isn't, or shouldn't be, about 'directing' anyone, but strictly about *accompanying* them, and in so doing, helping them to discover *for themselves* where God is active in their lives.

Spiritual companionship is at the heart of an individually given retreat. Such retreats, pioneered by the Jesuits in North America and in the UK, provide a space where a pilgrim can spend quality time with God, and also meet, usually daily, with a spiritual companion, to talk about what is happening for them, in the retreat and in their lives.

Individually given retreats are offered on a one-to-one basis, and may take place in the seclusion of a retreat centre, or in the pilgrim's normal daily-life situation.

Ignatian individually given retreats are based on the dynamic of Inigo's *Spiritual Exercises*, and, of course, those who so wish may make the full journey of the *Exercises*, with a companion who has had appropriate training to conduct this 'long' retreat. It is a long retreat because, to make the full *Exercises* in a residential setting takes at least 30 days, and to make the same intensive prayer journey in daily life (with meetings once a week or fortnight instead of once a day) can take up to nine months or even longer. It is a big commitment, but very few who undertake it remain unchanged by it.

So what are these *Exercises*? Basically, the *Spiritual Exercises* of St Ignatius are the notes that Inigo made about the inner movements he detected in himself, while he was in Manresa. They are his own 'retreat notes'. Although they appear in various printed forms, they are not meant to be read. They are an oral tradition, intended to be *given*, personally, by a companion to a pilgrim. They follow a set of structured scriptural (and a few very powerful nonscriptural) meditations, and ongoing guidance on how to discern in practice those movements in our lives that are of God, and those that are not – those that are leading us closer to what it means to be fully human, and those that are pulling us away, or distracting us from this goal. Once we can discern the difference, we can learn to nourish the positive movements and work against the negative.

The dynamic of the *Exercises* leads the pilgrim into deep reflection on the 'big questions':

- What is the shape of my life's story so far? Where is God in it?
- What is my life about now and where is it going?

- What is my deepest desire, and how do I envisage God's dream for me?
- Is anything blocking my relationship with God, with my deepest self, or with others?
- Where is my real security in life? Am I clinging to any false securities? If so, can I let them go?
- As I explore, more and more, the True Life, lived by Jesus of Nazareth, how do I want to respond?

Big questions, and a deep and powerful journey, in which the emphasis is always on discovering for ourselves where God is for us, and how we wish to respond – what personal part is ours to play in the ongoing human quest to become ever more fully human.

Do you have a 'soul friend', with whom you can really share your spiritual journey? Are you, or could you be, a soul friend for someone else? Have you ever considered making a retreat? If you would like an overview of the range of retreats available in the UK, have a look at the *Retreats* magazine, published annually by the Retreat Association, and available from most Christian bookshops.

Embodying – burning the candle at both ends

Not a good idea, normally. But suppose we substitute an oil lamp for the proverbial candle. An oil lamp, for me, is a wonderful icon of the Ignatian ideal of 'contemplation in action'. The wick has two ends. One end of the wick needs to be permanently immersed in the reservoir of oil. The other end needs to be sufficiently extended into the 'world' to be capable of being ignited. Provided both ends are in their proper place, the oil will seep up through the wick, and provide the fuel that enables the lamp to burn in the darkness.

Prayer is like that too. It is as though there is a wick running through the core of our being. One end of that 'wick' needs to be permanently immersed in God. This happens not just through deliberate times of prayer and meditation, or sustained retreats, but also in moment-by-moment reflective living. As we live each day, alive and alert, and observant of all that is happening, how we feel about it, how we react to it, and whether our reactions are adding to, or diminishing, the sum of trust, hope and love in the world, in all of this we are immersing our 'wick' in the oil of the presence of God. We are being faithful to the call of *contemplation*.

At the same time, we are called to live our lives in the real world, taking our full part in the drama of human life on earth. This demands our energy and engagement. Our 'wick' needs to be very much 'out there', and willing to be ignited and burned down over the years. This will only happen if the oil, our spiritual fuel, continues to rise up through the wick, to keep the flame alight. In our willingness to be, as it were, 'alight with God', and to let that light shine in life's darkest places, we are being faithful to the call to *action*.

It has been a Jesuit principle, from the beginning, to hold these two calls in balance, and to recognize that they are interdependent. Contemplation without action leaves the call to peace and justice unregarded. Action without contemplation will soon run out of fuel, and that fuel can only come from God.

An inspired and inspiring branch of Ignatian spirituality is the Christian Life Community (CLC), an association of mainly lay Christians who are quite consciously trying to live their lives by these principles, and by the dynamic of the

Ignatian *Exercises*. The CLC comprises large numbers of small local groups, all over the world, crossing the denominational divisions and affiliated to national and international organizations. A local group meets together regularly (perhaps every two weeks), to share what has been happening in their lives and help each other discern where God is active in them. For very many people, these groups are a way of deepening their Christian faith, and living it out in practice in very real and practical ways. Fellow pilgrims help each other know Christ better and discover what he is asking of them in their daily lives.

The CLC is, of course, just one way of giving practical expression to our desire to 'live true' following the Christian vision, and using the kind of tools we have been exploring in this book. Many people find that the support a group provides is invaluable in their daily-life discipleship. But underlying any form of discipleship is the question that keeps on and on presenting itself, in every event and encounter, every decision, every reaction: 'What is the more Christlike, the more loving, the more life-giving thing to do next in this situation?' To live in the constant tension of this question is to be seeking to embody the True Life, who is the Christ, in our own situations and circumstances.

What helps you to stay true to your Christian vision, and put it into practice? Do you have companions with whom you can share your faith journey? If not, and if you would welcome companionship, is there anything you can do to establish a small network of fellow pilgrims?

Another active and effective sign of Christian discipleship at its gospel-inspired best, is the growth of local groups of people who are passionate about issues of justice and peace.

They are often enthused with campaigning vigour, ready to speak out, and indeed, sometimes to suffer ridicule or worse, on behalf of those who have no voice in our societies. They are living out the call to be a catalyst for change, by challenging the sources and roots of our unjust economic, political and ecclesiastical systems. But not all engagement on behalf of justice and peace is high-profile. Simply to be present, with compassionate, yet challenging love, to an unjust, or oppressive situation in your own family, or community, or workplace, is often where it begins.

As you look around your own personal circumstances, where do you see unjust structures or movements? Is there anything you can do to challenge them, or to bring the influence of 'tough love' to bear upon them?

What 'cause' especially arouses your passion? Is there a group active on behalf of this cause in your locality? How might you add the gift of your passion and resources to such a group?

If you feel that your confrontation with injustice and oppression is too small to count, remember this: it often takes more courage to confront the oppressor in your own immediate situation than to take on the injustices of the wider world. Blessed are the peace-makers. God, the source of true peace, knows them, and empowers them.

The washing machine ate my clothes

And now for a little light relief . . .

My colleague, bless him, was a computer whiz-kid. He lived and worked, ate and breathed at the cutting edge of new computer technology and state-of-the-art software development. He was still young at the time and living in a bachelor pad, and he was one of the nicest guys I ever got to work with. But it has to be said that he wasn't the most practical man when it came to day-to-day necessities.

And so we find him, one evening after a long day at his computer screen, entering the launderette with a pile of washing. He duly places the washing inside an empty machine, reads the instructions, gets out the necessary coins, inserts them, selects the programme, and sets the machine in motion. He then sits down in front of the machine, to await the results, while he immerses himself in some erudite reading.

An hour or so later, the machine comes to the end of its cycle. With a sigh of satisfaction, he walks across, opens the door and gropes inside to extract his laundry. But there is nothing there! Absolutely nothing!

This mystery is altogether too much for him, especially at this advanced hour of the night. Is there something he doesn't know about washing machines? Are they capable of inflicting malicious damage on innocent laundry? Could the soap powder actually have *dissolved* his clothes? Or did some felon creep into the launderette, while he was busy with his Einstein, or whatever, and intercept his laundry in mid-cycle, making off with it into the night?

Perplexed, and not a little annoyed, he approaches the manager. 'The washing machine ate my clothes!' he complains, indicating the empty interior of the offending equipment. 'Well, that can't really be right, sir,' exclaims the manager, coming over to investigate the affair. And within a mere moment, the mystery is solved. My colleague had placed his washing in one machine, but inadvertently inserted the soap powder and coins into the adjacent machine, which had then duly washed its load of fresh air, while he waited patiently for it to finish. His dirty laundry was, of course, still sitting exactly where he had placed it.

It is a good story (and a true one), but it has a point as well, for our Christian discipleship. It is about making connections. If there is no connection between where you put your dirty washing, and where you put your soap and money, then nothing is going to happen, however assiduously the machine seems to be working. If there is no connection between the prayer we express with our mouths, and even in our hearts, and the place where we put our time, our energy, our resources and our passion, then nothing is going to change, however assiduously we pray that it should.

Love, as Ignatius insists, is shown in what we do, not just in what we say. If our spirituality becomes disconnected from our real-life situations, and the needs of our world and all the creatures who call it home, then the energy of the coming of the Kingdom will simply not be engaged. This is all completely obvious, of course. Truth so often is.

In this chapter we have looked at just a few of the ways we might explore in order to bring our desires and prayers into real and active connection with what we do. Not all of these ways are for all of us. Sometimes there will seem to be very little we can actually do in a particular situation, but that 'very little' may be the very thing that makes the difference. Our efforts may feel like a 'drop in the ocean', but what is the ocean if not a collection of 'drops'? Our little bit of loving may seem to make no difference to a broken world, but every compassionate act, every gentle word, every gesture of solidarity, every challenge to an unjust situation, is a drop in the ocean of God's love, and this ocean is the place where all creation lives, and moves, and has its being. It matters, very much, what kind of 'drops' we add to it.

7

More . . . ?

If you have read Charles Dickens's *Oliver Twist*, or seen the musical derived from it, you may remember the pathetic face of the hungry little orphan boy, Oliver, challenging the spartan regime of the workhouse to request a second helping of gruel. The response is not encouraging. 'More . . .?' bellows the director of the institution, and the word echoes back from all directions upon the hapless Oliver. '*More . . .?!* Are you expecting *more*?'

How dare we look for more? Aren't we supposed, as Christians, to be content with what we have? Why, then, does this little word 'more' (in Latin *magis*) keep threading its way through Inigo's *Exercises*, like a worm working through soil, continually making it better able to bear a rich harvest? We can't end our 'taster journey' into Ignatian spirituality without pausing to reflect on what Inigo might mean by this '*more*', and what this 'more' might mean for us, in our life pilgrimage.

More is less

There are two ways of looking at 'more'. One is about acquiring. The other is about relinquishing. It is easy enough to see how 'acquiring' can result in 'more'. We only need to wander through the shopping malls, and indulge in a little retail therapy, to know what it means to get caught up in the relentless drive of our generation to acquire more and more of what the consumer society has on offer. 'I shop, therefore I am'! Without even being aware of what is happening, we can slip into the great seduction of seeing ourselves, and others, in terms of what we possess.

These possessions don't have to come in any obviously 'material' form. We may feel we are quite restrained when it comes to surrounding ourselves with the luxuries and imagined necessities in the supermarkets and retail stores. We may live in relative simplicity. But there are other, more subtle ways of being acquisitive. We may be tempted to acquire symbols of our intellectual prowess, acquiring knowledge by devouring books or collecting qualifications, possibly without stopping to reflect on why we are doing so. We may express our deep hunger for love by entering into one relatively shallow relationship after another. We may even begin to pile up 'spirituality' in the same way, collecting more and more credentials of our spiritual worthiness. This is 'more', but it isn't the kind of 'more' we are invited to explore in the *Exercises*.

The other kind of 'more' is actually 'less'. It is about relinquishing things that are blocking our way to the pearl of great price. Perhaps as a child you played 'Pass the parcel'. If you remember, the game goes like this: A prize is wrapped up in many layers of wrapping paper and boxes, until it takes the form of a large parcel. The players sit in a circle, and pass the parcel from one to another while music is played. When the music stops the player who happens to be holding the parcel is allowed to begin unwrapping it, but may only continue until the music starts again, when the parcel must be relinquished. This process goes on, until eventually the last layer of wrapping is removed, and the prize is revealed. It is only a children's party game . . . But the truth it embodies is well worth exploring.

When the music stops

As long as the music plays, you have to keep on passing the parcel round. Just like life, really. As long as things are jogging along reasonably, most of our energy is spent, necessarily, on 'keeping things going'. There are jobs to be done, families to be raised, houses to be built, economies to be sustained and expanded. We are all in it together, one continuum of effort to maintain our own lives and the life of the world. No big traumas intervene, and the parcel passes smoothly from hand to hand.

But, of course, as we all know to our cost, the music *doesn't* keep on playing. We wake up one morning, and our health is shattered, our job has disappeared, a loved one has died, or walked away. Our certainties are crumbling and our trust has dissolved in the clouds of fear and anxiety.

It feels like the end of the world. But what if this is the very time and place to begin unwrapping the parcel? The parcel may feel like an onion. Peeling it only brings tears. All we really want is for the music to begin again. We want things to go back to how they were before our regulated lives were so rudely interrupted. In practice, however, and in God's greater wisdom, these times when the music stops may turn out to be the very places that lead us a bit closer to the pearl of great price, concealed under all the layers of our lesser desires and attachments. They may be invitations into the 'more'. When the old 'certainties' fall apart, the ruins may reveal new layers of the ground of our being.

It won't feel like this at the time, but just take a moment to think back:

> When has 'the music stopped' in your own life's story? Such times will usually have felt like some kind of diminishment. What happened at the time? As you

reflect back now with the benefit of hindsight, can you see any growth or deepening that resulted from the apparently unwelcome experience? Did your experience of 'less' lead you any closer to the 'more' at the core of your being, where God is indwelling? If there was some genuine treasure hidden for you beneath all the onion skins, what is it, and how do you feel about it now?

Asking for more . . . the Ignatian way

Given the kind of issues that we have been exploring in this book, and given the nature of the Christian gospel to upturn our expectations, it may not surprise you to hear the rather unlikely way Inigo has of 'asking for more'. This is how he expresses it:

> Take, Lord, and receive,
> my liberty,
> my memory,
> my understanding,
> my entire will,
> everything I have and call my own.
> You gave me every gift,
> And to you I return them.
> Use each one entirely according to your will.
> Give me only your love, and your grace,
> And that is enough for me.

What kind of a prayer is this? How could we possibly express these desires while in our right mind? Which of us is really willing to shed the protective layers of our rights of ownership, our freedom to do our own thing, the sovereignty of our own perceptions, judgements and choices? Is this really what Inigo is suggesting? Let's just unravel the layers a little.

On the face of it, expressing requests like these in prayer is either a sign of exaggerated asceticism, that negates much of what it means to be human, and devalues our autonomy, or it is the kind of 'I wish' prayer of surrender that we might speak with our lips but refuse to engage with in our hearts. I suggest Inigo's prayer (called the *Suscipe* prayer, from its first word in Latin) is neither of these things. Rather, it is an invitation to peel the onion, or unwrap the parcel, recognizing that this is the only way to discover the hidden treasure at the heart of things. In other words, we cannot discover the 'more' until, and unless, we are prepared to let go of the 'less'. It is a profound and extremely challenging prayer. If we enter into it sincerely, it draws us into an examination of what exactly the 'less' is, that is wrapped around the 'more'.

Peeling the onion

The nature of this 'less' will be different for each of us.

'My liberty' may look like the freedom to do as I want, but it may also be keeping me hovering at a superficial level of satisfaction, when my true contentment and my authentic growth will only come from accepting the constraints of what it means to be a member of an interdependent human family. The river flows deep and free because it flows between confining banks. Without them it would never reach its true destination, the ocean, but would turn into quagmire long before it reached the coast.

'My memory' may be trapping me in old resentments or outgrown ways of reacting to events, while my true self longs to move forward, and grow up. 'My memory' may

tell me that Aunt Jemima once insulted my parents: if I stay
with this memory, my grandchildren may never get to meet
their cousins, as the remembered injuries pass down through
the generations. Shedding this layer of the onion may sting
a few eyes, but it will leave the future free to smile again.

'My understanding and my entire will' may well appear,
to me, like the best thing since sliced bread, but they
may also be blinding me to the creativity and giftedness of
others. My 'I can do it my way' may be blocking the path-
ways leading to other, better ways. It has been truly said,
'the good is often the enemy of the better'.

'Everything I have and call my own' may take the form of
material possessions, but, more subtly, it may be a pointer
to emotional or spiritual possessiveness. We may have
become so involved in maintaining and extending our own
'kingdoms' that we have blocked off the way to the deeper
treasure. If you have ever spent a day searching for an
important document, and, in the process, wading through
mountains of old bills and letters accumulated through the
ages, you will know how hard it is to find what you really
need among all the clutter that you have hoarded. And that
is exactly how the pearl of great price gets lost – among the
mountains of lesser trinkets that you couldn't bear to throw
away.

These are just a few examples. Using Inigo's prayer as
a broad-brush guide, try peeling your own life's onion.
Is there anything that may be keeping you stuck
with the lesser good, and preventing you from moving
deeper to the hidden treasure at the core of your being?
Try to be specific in your reflections.

Jesus captures the very heart of the matter:

The Kingdom of heaven is like a treasure hidden in a field, which someone has found; he hides it again, goes off in his joy, sells everything he owns and buys it.

(*Matthew 13.44*)

What we are invited (not compelled) to surrender is actually the wrapping paper. Only when we are prepared to relinquish the wrapping will we discover the prize, and experience suggests that this process works better when the music stops than when everything is going to plan.

From 'please' to 'thank you'

When I was a small child, like most of my peers I tended to ask for what I wanted with scant regard for manners. My parents' response to my requests was often 'What else do you say?', to which the answer, of course, was 'please' or 'thank you'.

Our 'please' to God is like Oliver's request for 'more'. What about our 'thank you'? As we look back over our lives, or even over just one day, we will find so much to be grateful for. Our whole story, with all its ups and downs, and indeed the entire story of evolution, including its breakthroughs and its extinctions, has brought us to the place we find ourselves today. In one, still incomplete, lifetime, each of us has grown miraculously from a single cell into an adult human being, capable of speech and self-expression, creativity and imagination, empathy and love, and even able to reflect upon our own origin and destination. The process of our unfolding is awesome.

And so, at the end of his *Exercises*, Inigo invites us to reflect on how we are going to respond to all this gifting that has been pouring into us and through us for the last fifteen billion years of the existence of the universe we know today. What a question! How could anyone begin to respond to all of this? Even to think of 'paying it back' is ludicrous. But what about 'paying it forward'?

Paying it forward

I learned about 'paying it forward' on a Dublin bus. We had just landed in Dun Laoghaire, having changed our British currency into Euros. Banks being as efficient as they are, we had only a selection of crisp banknotes, and no small change. The bus driver on the 46A bus into Dublin City wasn't impressed. We would, he told us, not without Irish charm, have to get off the bus and find some small change – the *exact* small change – and then try again on the next bus into town.

We were about to follow these instructions when a young girl, boarding the bus behind us, reached across and gave the driver our exact fare, in the right coins. Amazed at this unexpected kindness, we thanked her profusely, but could do nothing at all to pay back this unwarranted generosity. As we travelled to town, enjoying the extra bonus of a lively conversation with her, a young man, sitting on the seat in front of her, turned round, having obviously witnessed the scene, and said he would also like to contribute to our fare, at which point he handed over a couple of Euros to the first girl. By this time we were drowning in embarrassment. It was a powerful lesson about how hard it is to accept gratuitous love, with no way of being able to repay it.

Once in town, and able to obtain some change, we salved our wounded consciences (or was it wounded pride?) by passing the bus fare on to the first homeless person we met. What was impossible to 'pay back' proved very easy to 'pay forward'.

I was recounting this episode afterwards, and someone told me about the film called *Paying It Forward*. Briefly, this film is about a challenge made to a class of children by their teacher, to 'find a way to make the world a better place'. One young boy comes up with the idea that every time something good happens to us, we should go out and do something good for three other people. When we can't return a favour, he reckons, we should 'pay it forward', threefold. This way, he calculates, the world would become vastly improved in a remarkably short time. He has not, of course, allowed for the rogue parameters of human greed, fear or sheer obstinacy.

While it was never likely to win any Oscars, this film does, nevertheless, shed useful light on the question of how we might respond to the gratuitous superabundance of the gifting we inherit, both personally, and as a whole human family – the gifting that shapes each unformed single cell into a full human being, capable of loving, laughing and relating, reflecting on the past and transforming the future. We can't pay anything back, because everything we have and are came gift-wrapped in that first single cell from which we grew. We possess nothing that has not been freely given to us. We don't have the right currency for 'paying it back' to God, but we *do* have the resources for 'paying it forward', to each other and the world.

We do this using the currency of love, hope and trust. Everything we do, every choice, every gesture, every reaction, has the potential to add to, or to diminish, the level of love, or of trust, or of hope in the world. We can choose to visit the sick neighbour, or ignore him. We can react to a critical comment with honesty or with anger. We can encourage others with our approach, or drag their spirits down with a negative remark.

The most harmful elements in our human living are not the infamous 'weapons of mass destruction' but the small but constant stabs of spite and malice we inflict on each other in polite conversations; the petty deprecations and diminishments that lower another person's self-esteem; the quiet passing-by on the other side of the silent cries of pain we don't want to hear.

The most life-giving elements of our human existence are not the heart transplants or moon shots. They are the unnoticed conversations with the lonely ones; the listening ear we offer to the hurting ones; the word of affirmation that lifts a veil of fear. These are the things that lie well within the range of our personal currency. How we spend that currency makes a great deal of difference.

> Try a little stock-taking today. Were there any opportunities to 'pay it forward'? How did you respond? Do you feel the world is a little richer in love, hope and trust tonight than it was this morning, as a result of your choices and responses to the day's events? No judgement allowed! Just notice what you see, and let it be there between you and God, allowing God to affirm and forgive as necessary.

Inheriting Inigo's legacy

We began with our imagination, as we flicked through some snapshots of Inigo's life, and we have, with Inigo's encouragement, allowed our imagination to shape our prayerful engagement with the Gospel narratives. It seems not unreasonable, therefore, to end our journey by imagining ourselves gathering round Inigo's death-bed, to make our personal farewell, to thank him for what he has given us as a guide to our Christian journeying, and to receive the legacy he leaves us.

No one can ever know what is really in the heart of another, much less presume to speak in another's name. So let this last section be strictly an imaginative exercise, offered from the point of view of just one twenty-first-century pilgrim in the Ignatian way, who ponders what the legacy of Ignatius Loyola means for spiritual searchers today. Receive Inigo's legacy in whatever way speaks to you. But don't put it away in some 'Sunday' cupboard. Try it on for size, and if it fits you – live it! Let's listen in to some of what the dying Ignatius might have wanted to say to those who would be inspired by his spirit, five centuries later.

'Jesus told us he is the *Way*. And so I want to leave you a way of walking that Way. It is a process of discovery, not a system of salvation. It is a Way that welcomes all who are seeking truth and love. It is a living Way, that moves and grows and changes, and illuminates every pathway you will ever walk, if you seek its light in prayer and reflection. It is the Way of Christ, and all it asks of you is to step out in trust, putting one foot in front of the other, and allowing yourself to be open to God's surprises round every corner.

'Native peoples have always known that God is in every particle of creation, as well as being the One who holds that creation in being. And so I want to leave you some signposts for discovering the living presence of God in absolutely every aspect of your life – in the world around you, the people whose lives touch yours, the work you do, the things you enjoy and the things that cause you pain, in the joy and the sorrow, the successes and the failures. I want you to discover for yourself that eternal presence in every moment, and the extraordinary revealed in the ordinary.

'Your own story matters. It is the unique thread of *you* that God is weaving into a tapestry none of us can begin to imagine. And so I want to leave you some ways, and some encouragement, to discover the meanings in your own life's story, and the ways in which God is revealing God's mystery through your history. I want to urge you to take your own story, and the stories of others, very seriously. They are chapters in the God-story. Your chapter of this story may last just three score years and ten, but it is a fragment of eternity, and without it, the full story cannot be told.

'I believed (and now I *know*) that the Christ-event that was revealed two thousand years ago is pivotal to the unfolding of God's mystery on planet earth. And so I leave you the gift of the Carpenter's workshop, where you can learn directly from Jesus what it means to be fully human, and how to put what you learn into practice in a world that longs for the fullness of its humanity, but can no longer see its way forward. I leave you a Christ-centred way of making your life's journey, and I commit you to the One who teaches you the skills, moment by moment.

'I was a practical man myself, and I follow a practical teacher, who walked through the world engaging with life hands-on. And so I leave you a very practical approach to Christian living, one that is workable and effective, addressing the real issues of your everyday life. I am hoping you will be both contemplative and active, in your journeying, keeping one end of your "wick" in the oil of prayer and reflective living, and the other courageously extended into the world where its light is so needed. I leave you my toolkit – my tried and tested ways of being a practical co-worker with Jesus of Nazareth, and making your own life choices in ways that embody his values and attitudes.

'Jesus lived a life of perfect balance, a life totally aligned with the true axis of God, around which all creation spins. And so I want to leave you some ways of discovering that kind of balance in your own life. I want to help you discover that when your heart is focused on what really matters most, then it won't be so terribly important whether you have a long life or a short one, whether you enjoy good health or not, whether you earn a lot or a little, or whether other people think highly of you or look down on you. To walk in this kind of balance will give you tremendous freedom, and I would love you to discover this gift in your own daily living.

'Jesus journeyed through life with companions. He chose to share his vision with a small circle of friends, and empowered them, in their turn, to do the same, so that the circles of love might grow to encompass all creation. I followed this model myself, and shared the gift God gave me with a small circle of companions. We called ourselves "Companions of Jesus". And so I want to leave you the gift of *companionship* on your journey of discipleship, in the living spirit of those first companions of Jesus, and all who have been inspired by the same vision since then, all down the centuries. Don't walk alone. God doesn't ask this of you. Walk with others and let others walk with you. Share your own vision and experience and be open to theirs, whether you do this in a small group of fellow pilgrims, or with just one or two chosen soul-friends, or in the wider community of believers, and of all who are searching for meaning in their lives.

'Jesus was a man for *everyone*. He didn't have favourites. He didn't cultivate the rich and powerful, though he didn't shun them either. And so I want to leave you a way of journeying with him that is *accessible* (whether you are an academic high flyer or someone who never even made it through primary school), and *inclusive* (whether you are a "pillar of the church" or an off-the-wall rebel). I want the way to be something you really understand, something that captures your imagination and inspires you to invest your energy in it. No one is excluded from this Christian journey – *no one*! It doesn't require educational qualifications – education gives you knowledge, but it is *experience* that gives you wisdom. Wisdom is what this journey is about. The source of your wisdom is your own experience, and experience is something that *everyone* has. My dearest wish for you is that you might come to *trust* your own experience, because that is where you will find God, and tap into your heart's deep wisdom.

'Jesus also described himself as the Truth, and he promised that truth will set us free. And so I want to leave you some ways of discerning what is really, deep down, true for you, and how to live true to the best in yourself. These tools are like two-edged swords, that will cut through the layers of falsehood that may be encrusting you, and are certainly encrusting our world and its ways of doing things. Learning to distinguish the true from the false, and the best from the merely "good", will be a painful process at times, but I am hoping that you will discover that it is nevertheless truly in line with what you most deeply desire.

'Back in the Basque country, all those years ago, I was given a gift beyond price. It started in Loyola with a shattered knee, and it continued in Manresa, and beyond, in my struggles with all that was darkest in my heart. Those were agonizing times, and yet they were the times and places when God felt closest, and touched me most profoundly. I can never repay God for this gift, but I can pay it forward . . . to *you*. I long for you too to discover for yourself that when life seems to be gouging out great holes in your heart, those same terrible gaping holes can become hollows that God will fill with grace you never dared to hope for. This grace will fill your own life and leave plenty to spare so that others may drink from these pools. I long for you to trust this process, to trust that, truly, less can be *more*.

'And so I entrust you to God's care and guidance, knowing that God will indeed forever beckon you beyond yourself, directing your vision and your energy towards others, towards God's world and all creation, and beyond every horizon in the quest to become who you most truly are.

'Journey with courage, journey with joy, journey with God, and in the constant companionship of Christ, the One who lives true.'

Appendix 1

To Take Your Ignatian Journey Further

You might like to contact one of the Ignatian spirituality centres that are run, under the direction of the Society of Jesus, in the UK and Ireland.

St Beuno's Ignatian Spirituality Centre,
St Asaph,
Denbighshire,
North Wales, LL17 0AS
+44(0)1745 583444
www.members.aol.com/StBeunos

Loyola Hall Spirituality Centre,
Warrington Road,
Rainhill,
Prescot,
Merseyside, L35 6NZ
+44(0)151 426 4137
www.loyolahall.co.uk

Ignatian Spirituality Centre,
7 Woodside Place,
Glasgow, G3 7QF
+44(0)14135 40077
www.iscentre.btinternet.co.uk

Manresa House Jesuit Spirituality Centre,
Dollymount,
Dublin 3,
Ireland
+00353(0)1 833 1352
www.jesuit.ie/manresa/contact.html

Other useful UK addresses

Christian Life Community,
St Joseph's,
Watford Way,
London, NW4 4TY
+44(0)20 82025 2555

The Jesuits in Britain,
114 Mount Street,
London, W1K 3AH
+44(0)20 7499 0285
www.jesuit.co.uk

The Retreat Association,
The Central Hall,
256 Bermondsey Street,
London, SE1 3UJ
+44(0)20 7357 7736
www.retreats.org.uk

Spiritual Exercises Network,
c/o John McGlinchey,
First Floor,
Champleys Mews,
Market Place,
Pickering,
North Yorkshire, YO18 7AE
01751 472 320
(for details of local Ignatian networks)

US addresses

Retreats International,
PO Box 1067,
Notre Dame,
IN 46556,
USA
(574) 247 4443
www.retreatsintl.org

Christian Life Community USA,
3601 Lindell Boulevard,
St Louis,
MO 63108,
USA
(314) 977 7370
www.clc-usa.org

The Cenacle Sisters website (for Open Door Retreats):
www.cenaclesisters.org

Society of Jesus USA,
US Jesuit Conference,
1616 P Street NW,
Suite 300,
Washington,
DC 20036-1420
USA
(202) 462 0400
www.jesuit.org

Appendix 2

References and Further Reading

Barry, William A., SJ, 1991, *Finding God in All Things*, Ave Maria Press, Notre Dame. A companion to the *Spiritual Exercises* of St Ignatius.

Bergan, J. S. and Schwann, M., 1991, *Praying with Ignatius of Loyola*, St Mary's Press, Winona, Minnesota.

Hughes, Gerard W., SJ, 1985, *God of Surprises*, Darton, Longman & Todd, London. Also available as a group package with accompanying cassette.

Hughes, Gerard W., SJ, 2003, *God in All Things*, Hodder & Stoughton, London.

Ivens, Michael, SJ, 1998, *Understanding the Spiritual Exercises*, Gracewing, Leominster. A guide for retreat directors.

Kolvenbach, Peter H., SJ, 1990, *Men of God, Men for Others*, St Paul Publications, Slough.

Lonsdale, David, 1992, *Dance to the Music of the Spirit: The Art of Discernment*, Darton, Longman & Todd, London.

Silf, Margaret, 1998, *Landmarks – An Ignatian Journey*, Darton, Longman & Todd, London.

Silf, Margaret, 2001, *Wayfaring – A Gospel Journey into Life*, Darton, Longman & Todd, London.

St Ignatius of Loyola, 1996, *Personal Writings*, translated and introduced by Joseph A. Munitiz and Philip Endean, Penguin Books, London.

Tetlow, Joseph, SJ, 1992, *Ignatius Loyola – Spiritual Exercises*, Crossroad, New York.

Young, William, SJ (trans.), 1980, *St Ignatius' Own Story*, Loyola University Press, Chicago. Autobiography, as told to Luis Gonzalez de Camara.